The Presidents of Congress

Before George

Joe Farrell • Lawrence Knorr • Joe Farley

SUNBURY PRESS
Mechanicsburg, PA USA

Published by Sunbury Press, Inc.
Mechanicsburg, PA USA

www.sunburypress.com

Copyright © 2024 by Joe Farrell, Joe Farley, and Lawrence Knorr.
Cover Copyright © 2024 by Sunbury Press, Inc.

Sunbury Press supports copyright. Copyright fuels creativity, encourages diverse voices, promotes free speech, and creates a vibrant culture. Thank you for buying an authorized edition of this book and for complying with copyright laws. Except for the quotation of short passages for the purpose of criticism and review, no part of this publication may be reproduced, scanned, or distributed in any form without permission. You are supporting writers and allowing Sunbury Press to continue to publish books for every reader. For information contact Sunbury Press, Inc., Subsidiary Rights Dept., PO Box 548, Boiling Springs, PA 17007 USA or legal@sunburypress.com.

For information about special discounts for bulk purchases, please contact Sunbury Press Orders Dept. at (855) 338-8359 or orders@sunburypress.com.

To request one of our authors for speaking engagements or book signings, please contact Sunbury Press Publicity Dept. at publicity@sunburypress.com.

FIRST SUNBURY PRESS EDITION: July 2024

Set in Adobe Garamond Pro | Interior design by Crystal Devine | Cover by Lawrence Knorr | Edited by Lawrence Knorr.

Publisher's Cataloging-in-Publication Data
Names: Farrell, Joe, author | Farley, Joe, author | Knorr, Lawrence, author.
Title: Before George : the presidents of Congress / Joe Farrell Lawrence Knorr Joe Farley.
Description: First trade paperback edition. | Mechanicsburg, PA : Sunbury Press, 2024.
Summary: Biographies of the various Presidents of the Continental Congress before the enaction of the US Constitution.
Identifiers: ISBN : 979-8-88819-250-4 (paperback).
Subjects: HISTORY / United States / Revolutionary Period (1775-1800) | BIOGRAPHY & AUTOBIOGRAPHY / Political.

Designed in the USA
0 1 1 2 3 5 8 13 21 34 55

For the Love of Books!

This book is dedicated to

WE HOLD THESE TRUTHS TO BE SELF-EVIDENT, that all men are created equal, that they are endowed by their Creator with certain unalienable Rights, that among these are Life, Liberty, and the pursuit of Happiness.—That to secure these rights, Governments are instituted among Men, deriving their just powers from the consent of the governed, —That whenever any Form of Government becomes destructive of these ends, it is the Right of the People to alter or to abolish it, and to institute new Government, laying its foundation on such principles and organizing its powers in such form, as to them shall seem most likely to effect their Safety and Happiness.

Contents

The Presidents of Congress.. 1

Peyton Randolph "The First President" 7
Henry Middleton "The Interim President"......................... 14
John Hancock "First President after Independence" 19
Henry Laurens "First President of the Recognized USA" 25
John Jay "The Diplomatic President"............................. 32
Samuel Huntington "First President of the Confederation"......... 43
Thomas McKean "First Elected President of the Confederation" 48
John Hanson "President During Yorktown"........................ 54
Elias Boudinot "President During the Treaty of Paris"............. 59
Thomas Mifflin "President Who Accepted Washington's Retirement"... 66
Richard Henry Lee "First President of the US Dollar"............. 71
Nathaniel Gorham "President at Shay's Rebellion" 77
Arthur St. Clair "First President of Westward Expansion"......... 81
Cyrus Griffin "The Last President of Congress" 88
Charles Thomson "The Secretary of Congress"..................... 94

Appendix A: Terms of the Presidents of Congress................. .99
Appenix B: The Articles of Confederation Regarding the
    Role of the President...................................... .100
Sources... 101
Index 105

The Presidents of Congress

For many years, historians have largely dismissed the role of the President of Congress during the American Revolution as too unlike the later post-Constitution President of the United States to bear comparison. We count the Presidents from George Washington onward. Who else could have been the first *real* President of the United States but our great Commander in Chief of the Continental Army? For that reason alone, it seems almost sacrilegious to suggest otherwise. But, taking the wider view, if you consider the progression of the creation of our central government from a loose collaboration of rebellious colonies to a union of states with a federal capital, the role of the President of Congress becomes more interesting.

Considering the First Continental Congress, when the delegates arrived in Philadelphia in September of 1774 in response to the Intolerable Acts, the Revolutionary War had not yet begun. Lexington and Concord were not even a thought—they were months away. The great controversy to be discussed was a problem in and around Boston where tea had been thrown in the bay, and the British were now clamping down. This First Continental Congress was without a charter or constitution. The delegates arrived to show solidarity with Massachusetts and one another. They intended to discuss and decide on a collective course of action, most wanting to avoid outright confrontation. Immediately, they organized themselves loosely by selecting a presiding officer, officially the President of the United States in Congress Assembled acting as a parliamentarian for the discussions, and a Secretary tracking the quorums, proposals, and decisions.

During this nascent period of proto government, the Congress elected from their midst someone to moderate their discussions. At this

The First Continental Congress prays for guidance.

moment, they were all individual colonies with their own colonial assemblies. The collaboration in Philadelphia was not seen as a superior federal organization but rather a temporary interaction to make a collective response. The result was the Continental Association coordinating trade embargos with the mother country. Following its signing, the Congress disintegrated and went home.

Then came the "Shot Heard Round the World." After shots were fired between colonial militiamen and British regulars in Massachusetts, the war was on. Congress was once again called to Philadelphia, and the Second Continental Congress assembled with more urgency. Now, there was the gravitas of military action and the discussion of foreign alliances. There were also the rumblings of cries for outright independence. Initially, the so-called Oliver Branch Petition was agreed to and sent to King George III, but it was rebuffed. Then, the following year, the Declaration of Independence. During this period, the presiding officer of the Congress carried more weight, especially from the Declaration onward. The discussions were more serious, and the need for more collaboration increased. However, the lack of a constitution and the chaos of herding thirteen colonies made progress difficult. At this point, while the president and

The Second Continental Congress discusses independence.

secretary were not writing the decisions of Congress and answering letters directly, they were signing them to make them official. When the Declaration of Independence was passed, it was the President of Congress, John Hancock, who signed it most prominently, followed by the Secretary of Congress, Charles Thomson, even though he was not a delegate.

As the war progressed, often poorly, the Congress debated the creation of a more formal arrangement between them. This ultimately became the Articles of Confederation. However, the role of the President of Congress had not changed very much. There was concern about creating too strong a central figure for the government at a time when they were battling a tyrannical monarchy. For this reason, the president's term was now limited to one year, and he could not serve more than once every three years. But the President of Congress was now privy to all the business of the Congress, including the secret communications with foreign governments and alliances with France and the Netherlands. In practice, he functioned similarly to a speaker of the house.

Following the victory over Britain and the negotiation of peace, the Continental Congress became a less desirable place to spend time as a delegate from one of the states. It was far more prestigious to be a speaker of a colonial house of representatives, a governor, or a judge on a state supreme court than it was to be the President of Congress, which had no authority to tax and lead the nation. During this period, the

Before George

president and secretary were the only two continuously serving members of the young government. It was quickly becoming clear the young nation needed a more formal arrangement; thus, the Constitutional Convention was held, and a new Constitution was passed that better defined the role of the federal government. Rather than one house of representatives, the new government had two houses and three co-equal branches. The need for a stronger executive leader was now understood. While this role, as its predecessor, could not write the laws, pass them, or raise money, the executive signed the documents or vetoed them and was also the commander in chief of the military. He was also in charge of his own cabinet at a time when there were no federal departments to manage. Essentially, the role handed to George Washington was vastly expanded from that of the President of Congress with a clear role with the military, fitting Washington to a tee. The role of the new Vice President of the United States bore a closer resemblance to the President of Congress as an executive officer with no clear duties except to preside over the Senate.

During the many months when the Constitution was being ratified in the various states, the waning President of Congress had less and less to do. He and the secretary were in charge of shutting down the prior

The Committee of Five stands before President Hancock and Secretary Thomson at the passage of the Declaration of Independence.

government and transitioning to the new, even at a time when few delegates arrived to serve.

The men who served as President of Congress, often reluctantly, were all Patriots who risked their lives as traitors against the Crown. Their signatures on the rebels' official documents made them targets. This book delves into the biographies of these men, focusing on the entirety of their lives and not just their brief moments as the lead parliamentarians. For some, however, there were great or historic moments:

Peyton Randolph was the first presiding officer of the Congress.

John Hancock was the President of Congress at the time of the Declaration of Independence. Some could argue he was the very first President of the United States as a (declared) independent nation.

Henry Laurens was in the seat when the Articles of Confederation were discussed and the French alliance was established.

Samuel Huntington was in the role when the Articles of Confederation were ratified and put into effect.

Thomas McKean was the President of Congress at the time of the victory at Yorktown.

John Hanson was the first to serve the proscribed one-year term under the Articles of Confederation at a time when the nation had earned its independence. One could argue John Hanson was the first President of the United States as a free and independent nation.

Elias Boudinot was in the role at the time of the Treaty of Paris.

Thomas Mifflin was the President who accepted the retirement of George Washington as Commander in Chief following the victory.

Arthur St. Clair was in charge at the beginning of the Constitutional Convention and helped establish the Northwest Territory, where he soon became governor.

Lastly, Cyrus Griffin was the transitional figure from the old government to the new, a thankless job.

Throughout this entire period, the one constant was Secretary of Congress, Charles Thomson. He served continuously and was often the only officer in place during interim periods when there was no President or when Congress was not in session. In the end, when only two delegates arrived in Philadelphia, achieving a quorum was next to impossible, and Thomson, in Griffin's absence, was the caretaker.

George Washington relinquishes his role as commander in chief to President Thomas Mifflin.

In summary, these men all played important roles in the governance of our young nation during its most formative stages. As the rebellious colonies loosely collaborated with the assistance of a reluctant parliamentarian, it became apparent, albeit slowly, that better leadership would be required. Over time, as the colonies transitioned to a war footing and declared independence, the role of the President of Congress became much more serious, albeit lacking authority. The Articles of Confederation then did little to improve the situation except to make it official and to be sure there would be no tyrant in charge. It was the creation and ratification of the United States Constitution that recognized the need for a strong executive with military responsibilities. The only common thread along the way was the use of the title President of the United States. Today, in an era of governing a global superpower with an immense bureaucracy, quite a bit of which falls under the auspices of the executive branch and its cabinet members and their departments, the powers of the current occupant of the Oval Office are unimaginably greater from the first few Presidents of the United States in the Constitutional era, illustrating the continuing evolution of this important role.

Lawrence Knorr (2024)

Peyton Randolph
(1721–1775)

"The First President"

Buried at Wren Chapel at the College of William and Mary,
Williamsburg, Virginia

Continental Association

Peyton Randolph was the Attorney General and Speaker of the House of Burgesses in colonial Virginia prior to the American Revolution. He was early to the Patriot cause despite his connections to the colonial government. He was elected to both the First and Second Continental Congresses and served as the first President of those bodies. As such, he signed the Continental Association.

Randolph, born on September 10, 1721, at Tazewell Hall in Williamsburg, Virginia, the son of Sir John Randolph and his wife, Susannah (née Beverly or Beverley) Randolph. The Randolphs were wealthy plantation owners, and Sir John was a barrister who also served as Speaker of the House of Burgesses from 1734 to 1736 and as the Virginia colony's Attorney General. Sir John's father had also been the Speaker of the House, and the family had a long history of public service back to Sir Thomas Randolph (1523–1590), who was an advisor to Queen Elizabeth I.

Randolph had two brothers and one sister. The eldest brother, Beverley Randolph (1719–1764), married Agatha Wormeley (1721–1786) in 1742. Sister Mary Randolph (1720–1768) married Colonel

Before George

Peyton Randolph

Philip Ludwell Grymes (1721–1761), a member of the Virginia House of Burgesses, in 1742. The younger brother, John Randolph (1727–1784), married Ariana Jennings in 1750.

Sir John died in 1736, when Randolph was only 15, leaving the four children with their widowed mother. Soon after, Randolph attended the College of William and Mary in Williamsburg but did not graduate. In late 1739, he traveled to England to study law at the Middle Temple of Gray's Inn, a prominent law school. On February 10, 1744, after completing his studies, he was accepted by the London bar.

Randolph returned to Virginia and, in 1746, married Elizabeth Harrison of the Berkeley plantation, the sister of Benjamin Harrison, who would later sign the Declaration of Independence and be the grandfather and great-great-grandfather of two presidents. Peyton and Elizabeth had no children and lived on Nicholson Street in Williamsburg.

Based on a recommendation of John Hanbury, an English friend, Randolph was appointed the Attorney General for Virginia in 1748, despite the reservations of Royal Governor William Gooch. Randolph was also elected to the House of Burgesses.

In 1753, Randolph became embroiled in a dispute with Royal Governor Robert Dinwiddie when he was asked by the House of Burgesses to travel to England at the government's expense, including his salary, to oppose a land patent fee imposed by the governor before the British Board of Trade. The fee would be charged to colonists wishing to expand their land holdings. Normally, as Attorney General, Randolph was to represent the governor rather than the legislature. The governor and his council were outraged and replaced Randolph with George Wythe. Randolph arrived in London near the end of 1754 but was unable to sway the Board. However, when Randolph returned in a few months, the governor reinstated him, and the fee was dropped. This was an early instance of the colonists protesting taxation from overseas.

Following Braddock's defeat in 1755, Randolph led the "Associators," 300 militiamen who rallied to defend Virginia. On May 3, 1756, he wrote Colonel George Washington:

> Some public-spirited Gentlemen have done me the honor to fix upon me as their leader till we can come to the place where you command, when we shall be very glad to follow such orders, as you shall think most conducive to the public good.

After the French and Indian War in 1765, when Parliament was attempting to recoup the cost of the war from the colonists via the Stamp Act, the Virginia House of Burgesses selected Randolph to draft a petition to the King opposing it. Patrick Henry had raised his own objections to the Act, and most of them were accepted, superseding Randolph's more conservative petition. The amended petition was ignored by the King, and the tax was imposed.

This roiling of the colonial powers put Randolph in a position of disfavor with the governor. As he became Speaker of the House in 1766 following the death of John Robinson, he resigned from the Attorney General position and was replaced by his brother John, a Loyalist. Randolph then focused on his role in the House of Burgesses, leading a committee to collect and revise the laws of the colony in 1769. Said Thomas Jefferson of Randolph's performance as Speaker:

Before George

Altho' not eloquent, his matter was so substantial that no man commanded more attention; which, joined with a sense of his great worth gave him a weight in the House of Burgesses which few ever attained.

In reaction to the discontent regarding the Townshend Acts (1767), Governor Lord Botetourt dissolved the House of Burgesses on May 17, 1769. Randolph and other members walked to Raleigh Tavern and formed an Association, which ultimately led to non-importation agreements and boycotts of English goods. Randolph led this opposition and also issued a statement of support for the Boston Port Act in 1773 as chair of the new Committee of Correspondence.

On September 5, 1774, Randolph, George Washington, Benjamin Harrison, Edmund Pendleton, Richard Henry Lee, Patrick Henry, and Richard Bland were sent to Philadelphia as delegates to the First Continental Congress. Randolph was nominated to the President of the Congress and was unanimously approved. The Congress asked for the repeal of the Coercive Acts and signed the Continental Association. Randolph then resigned as President, to head back to Virginia. He was replaced by Henry Middleton after a term of forty-seven days.

Following Patrick Henry's "give me liberty or give me death" speech in March 1775, at which Randolph presided, Royal Governor Lord Dunmore had the Royal Marines remove the gunpowder and muskets from the armory in Williamsburg on April 21, 1775. Unknown to anyone at the time, the first shots had been fired at Lexington and Concord. Randolph and the Associators were angered by this, and Patrick Henry threatened a military response. Carter Braxton helped to negotiate a payment for the arms from the governor to avoid a confrontation.

The Second Continental Congress was called on May 10, 1775, and Randolph was once again elected its President. However, in June, when Lord Dunmore called the House of Burgesses back in session, Randolph resigned from Congress and headed home. Thomas Jefferson took his seat in Congress, and John Hancock became President. As the Speaker of the Virginia House, Randolph rejected the offer of reconciliation from Lord North, who was trying to divide the colonies by reconciling with

Peyton Randolph (1721–1775)

The crypt under the Wren Chapel at the College of William and Mary containing the grave of Peyton Randolph.

them individually. The Continental Congress rejected it as well. As Lord Dunmore fled that June, Randolph led the formation of a Committee of Safety.

When the Continental Congress met again in Philadelphia in September 1775, Randolph returned as a delegate despite being in ill health. John Adams was concerned that Randolph might want his seat back as President when he wrote that Randolph "Sits very humbly in his Seat, while our new [President] continues in the Chair, without Seeming to feel the Impropriety." On October 22, 1775, while dining with Thomas Jefferson, Randolph suffered a five-hour-long "fit of apoplexy" and died. Said one Philadelphia newspaper (likely Franklin's):

> Last Sunday died of an apoplectic stroke, in the fifty-third year of his age, the Hon. Peyton Randolph, Esq; of Virginia, late President of the Continental Congress, a general who possessed the virtues of humanity in an eminent degree, and joining with them the

Before George

The approximate location in the Wren Chapel under which is Randolph's crypt.

soundest judgment, was the delight of his friends in private life, and a most valuable member of society, having long sided, and with great . . . integrity discharged the most honourable public trusts.

The entire Congress attended his funeral in Philadelphia on October 24, 1775. Carter Braxton was then called as a replacement for the Virginia delegation in Congress. Randolph's body was returned to Williamsburg and buried in the vault beneath the chapel at the College of William and Mary. When he died, in addition to his house in Williamsburg, Randolph also owned several pieces of land in town, two plantations in James City County, and more than 100 slaves.

Peyton Randolph (1721–1775)

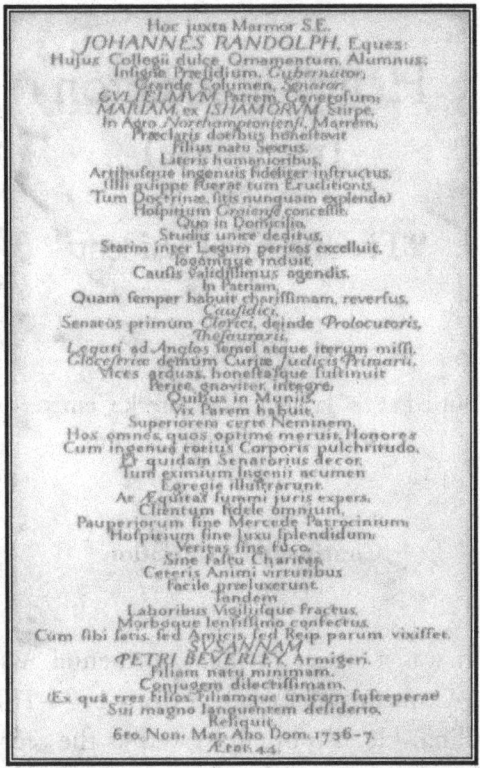

The memorial plaque in the Wren Chapel dedicated to the Randolphs.

In honor of Randolph, the Congress named one of the first naval frigates the USS *Randolph* and a fort on the Ohio River as Fort Randolph. Randolph County, North Carolina; Randolph, Massachusetts; and Randolph County, Indiana, were named to his honor. During World War II, the aircraft carrier USS *Randolph* was named for him. The Peyton Randolph House in Colonial Williamsburg was declared a National Historic Landmark in 1970.

In October 1859, there was a fire in the chapel area of the college. Randolph's was the only vault damaged, but the newspaper reported his coffin was in excellent condition.

Henry Middleton
(1717 – 1784)

"The Interim President"

Buried at St. James Goose Creek Cemetery,
Goose Creek, South Carolina

Continental Association

Henry Middleton was a signer of the Continental Association during his service in the Continental Congress from 1774-1776 as a delegate from South Carolina. He also briefly served as the second President of Congress. Middleton was a wealthy plantation owner and the father of Declaration of Independence signer Arthur Middleton. However, after the fall of Charleston in 1780, he reaffirmed his loyalty to the king and remained a British subject until his death in 1784.

Middleton was born on his father Arthur Middleton's plantation, "The Oakes" near Charleston, South Carolina, in 1717. He was the son of Arthur and Sarah (née Amory) Middleton. The Middleton line had likely originated near Derbyshire, England, as far back as Queen Elizabeth I. Arthur (the elder) served in the colonial government including rising to acting governor. Middleton was likely taught by private tutors at home before going to England to complete his education.

During his younger years, Middleton served as a justice of the peace and later was elected to the colonial Commons of the Hour of Assembly, representing his St. George's County. In 1754, he was elected Speaker of

Henry Middleton (1717–1784)

Portrait of Henry Middleton by Benjamin West, circa 1771.

this body and was later named as a member of His Majesty's Council for the Province of South Carolina.

Middleton married Mary Baker Williams with whom he had a dozen children, seven of whom survived childhood. Upon marrying Mary Williams in 1741, the daughter of John Williams, also a wealthy plantation owner, Middleton received a dowry which included the plantation that would become "Middleton Place." He and the family lived there until Mary's death in 1761, at which time he moved back to "The Oakes" and gave "Middleton Place" to his son Arthur. After Mary died, he married Mary Henrietta Bull, the daughter of William Bull, who had been the Lieutenant Governor of South Carolina. She died in 1772. The two had no children together, Middleton last married Lady Mary McKenzie in 1776.

Early on, Middleton was against the Stamp Act, and by 1770 had declined to continue serving on His Majesty's Council. In 1774, he was elected to the first Continental Congress, representing South Carolina along with John Rutledge, Christopher Gadsden, Thomas Lynch, and Edward Rutledge, Middleton attended the entire first Continental

Before George

Congress and into the second, until early 1776 when he became ill and was replaced by his son Arthur. Middleton had also been elected President of Congress for a brief period, October 22 to 26, in 1775 while Peyton Randolph was unable to serve. However, some records seem to indicate he might have served longer, starting earlier in October. A petition to Ben Franklin and others had been signed by Middleton, as President of Congress, as early as October 6.

During his service, Middleton had been instrumental in establishing a new government for South Carolina and was well-respected by others for his willingness to negotiate with the King as opposed to leaping right to independence like others from the northern colonies. In this regard, he differed from his son, who was a staunch voice for independence. Middleton resigned from his position in the Congress and returned to "The Oakes" prior to the Declaration of Independence due to declining health. His son signed the document instead.

As one of the leaders of the revolt against British rule, Middleton came to the attention to the British authorities, who ordered his arrest and execution. From a letter from the Earl of Dunmore from London, 30 January 1775:

> From unquestionable authority I learn, that about a fortnight ago, dispatches were sent hence by a sloop of war to General [Thomas] Gage, containing, among other things, a Royal Proclamation, declaring the inhabitants of Massachusetts Bay and some others, in the different Colonies, actual rebels; with a blank commission to try and execute such of them as he can hold of . . . with this is sent a list of names, to be inserted in the commission as he may judge expedient. I do not know them all, but Messrs. Samuel Adams, John Adams, Robert Treat Paine, and John Hancock, of Massachusetts Bay; John Dickinson, of Philadelphia; Peyton Randolph, of Virginia, and Henry Middleton, of South Carolina, are particularly named, with many others. This blacklist, the General will, no doubt, keep to himself, and unfold it gradually, as he finds it convenient.

Henry Middleton (1717 – 1784)

The graves of Henry Middleton's daughter Susannah Middleton and her husband Continental Congressman John Parker at St. James Goose Creek Cemetery in Goose Creek, South Carolina. The location of Henry's grave is not known, but it may be close to this one. Based on the old etching, there was a tombstone next to it that no longer exists. (photo by Lawrence Knorr).

Back in South Carolina, during the period between royal rule and statehood, Middleton was a member of the state Legislative Council, which helped to form South Carolina. In 1778 he was elected to the South Carolina state Senate, where he served until 1780.

When Charleston fell to the British in 1780, Middleton was faced with financial ruin and certain execution. Rather than face such an end, he paid off the British invaders and reaffirmed his loyalty. Subsequently, his estates were not further touched, though his son's was burned to the ground and ransacked.

Middleton's health continued to decline over the following years. He died in Charleston on June 13, 1784, after a long illness. He was laid to rest at St. James Goose Creek cemetery at "Goose Creek," one of the Middleton family estates, located in Berkeley County, South Carolina. In all, through purchases and other means, Middleton, by the time of his death, had accumulated some 50,000 acres of land, a total of 50 estates and plantations, and approximately 800 slaves, becoming one of the wealthiest men in South Carolina prior to and during the American Revolution.

Apparently, his reversal of loyalty did not diminish the opinions held of him locally due to his many contributions early in the fight for independence and the role played by his son, Arthur. His estates were not confiscated as were many loyalists following the war.

John Hancock
(1737–1793)

"First President after Independence"

Buried at Granary Burial Ground,
Boston, Massachusetts

Declaration of Independence • Articles of Confederation • Governor

John Hancock must have been an unusual and remarkable person. He inherited enormous wealth, was educated, nice looking, popular, living a wonderful life, and yet he was willing to risk it all in the cause of the American Revolution. He contributed immensely to our nation's founding in many ways, including serving in the Continental Congress, twice as President of Congress, and as a signer of the Declaration of Independence. His signature on that document was so bold that when people sign their names, they are said to have written their "John Hancock."

John Hancock was born on his family's farm in Braintree, now Quincy, Massachusetts, on January 23, 1737. His father, John, was a minister and died when young John was seven. He was adopted by his uncle Thomas Hancock, one of Boston's wealthiest merchants, and his aunt Lydia (Henchman) Hancock. Young John lived in an elegant mansion on Beacon Hill called Hancock Manor and was sent to the elite Boston Latin School. He graduated in 1750 and enrolled in Harvard. He received his bachelor's degree from Harvard in 1754 at the age of 17. He then entered his uncle's shipping business. In 1760 he moved to England while building relationships with customers and suppliers. He returned

Before George

John Hancock

in 1761 and soon became a partner in the company, House of Hancock. When Thomas Hancock died of a stroke in August 1764, John inherited the business, Hancock Manor, two or three slaves, and thousands of acres of land, becoming one of the colonies' wealthiest men. The slaves were eventually freed through the terms of Thomas's will. John developed a reputation for generosity, but his lavish lifestyle had its critics, including Sam Adams.

In 1765 the British Parliament enacted the Stamp Act tax on the colonies, and it was a catalyst for John Hancock. He became involved in politics protesting regulations like the Stamp Act and Townshend Act. He commandeered public acts of protest and joined in support of a boycott of British goods. To avoid British taxes, Hancock allegedly began smuggling goods aboard his vessels. This made him very popular among the locals, and in 1766 he was elected to the Massachusetts House of Representatives.

John Hancock (1737–1793)

Hancock came into direct conflict with the British in 1760, when one of his merchant ships, the *Liberty*, was seized in Boston Harbor by British customs officials who claimed Hancock had illegally unloaded cargo without paying the required taxes. Being a popular figure, the seizure of his ship led to angry protests by residents. He was taken to court and given a huge fine. It was not the first time Hancock had friction with the Customs Board. Many thought they harassed Hancock because of his politics. He hired John Adams to defend him, and eventually, the charges were dropped without explanation. His guilt or innocence is still debated. Hancock became a local hero for standing up to the British authorities. One result of all this was Hancock and Sam Adams emerged as political partners. Adams was a rabble-rousing firebrand who was hated by the British. He and Hancock, along with James Otis, Paul Revere, and others, formed a grassroots group named the Sons of Liberty. Thus, Hancock became increasingly involved in the movement for American independence, and Massachusetts was at the center of the movement. Boston was dubbed the "Cradle of Liberty."

A result of all the unrest in Boston was a show of military might. Four regiments of the British army were sent to Boston to support the royal officials. The tension between the soldiers and civilians led to what became known as the Boston Massacre in March 1770, in which five civilians were killed and six wounded by British troops. Hancock headed a committee that met with Governor Thomas Hutchinson and demanded the removal of British troops from Boston. He claimed that there were 10,000 armed colonists ready to retaliate if the troops did not leave. The troops being in a precarious position were moved to Castle William, and Hancock was celebrated as a hero reflected in his near-unanimous reelection to the House of Representatives.

Boston became a volatile site once again with the passage of the Tea Act of 1773. Although Hancock did not participate in the Boston Tea Party, he was present at the December 16, 1773, meeting preceding the dumping of the tea and approved of the action. On March 5, 1774, Hancock delivered an important speech on the Boston Massacre's fourth anniversary, denouncing British troops' presence in Boston and questioning Britain's authority over the colonists' lives. The speech was published and widely distributed, enhancing Hancock's stature as a leading Patriot.

Before George

In May of 1774, Governor Hutchinson was replaced by Thomas Gage. Whereas Hutchinson tried to win over Hancock, believing that he was too influenced by Sam Adams, Gage took a hard line against both men. In December 1774, Hancock was elected president of the Massachusetts Provincial Congress, which declared itself an autonomous government. Later that month, he was chosen as a delegate to the Second Continental Congress, which served as the colonies' governing body.

Hancock was in the middle of several of the most important events of early American history. He was in Lexington, Massachusetts, on April 18, 1775, when Paul Revere rode his horse to warn fellow colonists that the British were on the move toward Boston. Hancock was with Sam Adams when they heard the alarm. Both men were targeted for arrest by the British. The advance warning allowed them to flee and ultimately escape and make their way to Philadelphia to attend the Continental Congress that convened on May 10. On May 24, Hancock was elected as the third President of the Continental Congress.

When the congress adjourned in August, Hancock made his way to Fairfield, Connecticut, where he wed his fiancée, Dorothy (Dolly) Quincy, on August 28. John and Dolly would have two children, Lydia, who died at ten months, and John George Washington Hancock, who died at nine from a head injury while ice skating.

Hancock was President of Congress when the Declaration of Independence was adopted and signed. He was the first person to sign the historical document and did so with a large, flamboyant signature. According to legend, he signed largely and clearly so that King George could read it without his spectacles.

In October 1777, Hancock told the Continental Congress that he would be resigning the presidency and returning to Massachusetts for health reasons. He had fallen out of favor with both Adamses, who disapproved of Hancock's vanity and extravagance. Many doubted he resigned for health reasons. He rejoined Congress in June 1778, and on July 9, joined representatives from seven other states in signing the Articles of Confederation and then returned to Boston.

Hancock had his chance for military glory shortly after when he led nearly six thousand soldiers to recapture Newport, Rhode Island, from the British. It was a complete failure. He suffered some criticism for the failed attempt but emerged with his popularity intact.

After returning to Massachusetts, Hancock desired to stay in the public eye. As the state needed funds to pay soldiers and purchase weaponry, he used his personal funds to assist in these areas. He also handed out food and firewood to the poor at his own expense. According to biographer William Fowler, "John Hancock was a generous man and the people loved him for it. He was their idol."

The new Massachusetts constitution, which Hancock helped frame, went into effect in October 1780. He was the first democratically elected Governor of Massachusetts in a landslide, garnering over ninety percent of the vote. He remained governor until his surprise resignation in 1785. He again cited health reasons, but some critics claim he wanted to avoid a difficult situation. Historian James Truslow Adams wrote that Hancock's "two chief resources were his money and his gout, the first always used to gain popularity and the second to prevent his losing it." The turmoil Hancock avoided was Shay's Rebellion, which his successor, James Bowdoin, had to deal with. In 1786, after nearly two years out of office, Hancock ran again and defeated Bowdoin and pardoned all the rebels. Hancock was reelected to annual terms as governor for the remainder of his life.

He did not attend the 1787 Constitutional Convention but did preside over Massachusetts's 1788 convention to ratify the Constitution and gave a speech in favor of it. Even with the support of Hancock and Sam Adams, the convention narrowly ratified it by a vote of 187 to 168.

In his ninth term as governor, he reconciled with his old friend Sam Adams and in his final election as governor, Adams served as his running mate and as lieutenant governor.

In 1789 Hancock was a candidate in the first U.S. Presidential election. He received four electoral votes out of a total of 138 cast. Following a lengthy illness, John Hancock died at his home with his wife at his side on October 8, 1793, at 56 years of age. After a lavish funeral, he was laid to rest in the Old Granary Burying Ground in Boston, where the Boston Massacre victims are also buried. A large obelisk-shaped stone marks his grave.

The monument to John Hancock.

Henry Laurens
(1724–1792)

"First President of the Recognized USA"

Laurens Family Cemetery
Moncks Corner, Berkeley County, South Carolina

Articles of Confederation

Henry Laurens was a South Carolina plantation owner, merchant, and partner in the largest slave-trading house in North America. Laurens was active in state and national politics as the Vice President of South Carolina, Continental Congressman, and President of Congress. He signed the Articles of Confederation, presiding over its adoption. He was also the Minister to the Hague during the Revolution but was captured by the British on his return and imprisoned in the Tower of London for fifteen months.

Laurens, born on March 6, 1724, in Charleston, South Carolina, was the eldest son and third child of Jean Samuel Laurens and Hester (née Grasset) Laurens. His father was of French Huguenot descent, arriving with his parents in New York in the late 1600s. About 1715 or 1716, the elder Laurens married a French Huguenot wife from Staten Island; the young couple moved to Charleston, South Carolina, where Henry was born a decade later. Mother Hester Laurens died in 1741, and her husband remarried Elizabeth Wickling. Jean Samuel Laurens then passed in 1747, leaving his estate to his eldest son, Henry.

Before George

Henry Laurens

Laurens was initially educated in Charleston. In 1744, at age 19, he went to England to study business with Richard Oswald, the principal owner of Bunce Island, a slave-trading island base in the Sierra Leone River of Africa. He stayed there until his father's death three years later.

Leveraging his inheritance, Laurens quickly rose as a leader of the merchant class in Charleston, trading with England and the West Indies. His plantation on the Cooper River employed over 300 slaves, and he was an active importer and trader of slaves throughout the colonies.

On June 25, 1750, Laurens married Eleanor Ball, the daughter of a South Carolina rice planter. The couple had thirteen children, most of them dying in childhood. During the 1750s, Laurens held local offices and, in 1757, was elected to the Commons House of Assembly, staying there through the beginning of the Revolution in 1775, except for 1773, when he arranged his sons' education in England.

From 1757 to 1761, Laurens was also a lieutenant colonel in the militia, fighting a campaign against the Cherokee during the French and Indian War. During the spring of 1760, smallpox raged throughout the low country of South Carolina. Lauren's infant daughter, Martha, apparently succumbed to the disease. As was customary, her little body was laid on a bed by an open window. The family then gathered around for a wake for the deceased. Outside, a light rain began to fall, and a cool breeze blew a few droplets on the young girl's head. She began to stir, clearly not dead. The child had narrowly avoided being buried alive! Little Martha recovered, married Dr. David Ramsay, and lived a full life.

In 1764 and 1768, Laurens was named to the King's Council of South Carolina but declined. Wife Eleanor died in 1770 of complications from the childbirth of their last child. Laurens left his local offices to care for his children and then, realizing the harsh impacts of British trade policies, traveled to London to attempt to unsuccessfully negotiate a resolution.

In 1772, Laurens joined the American Philosophical Society of Philadelphia and became well-acquainted with the other members. In 1773, on the eve of the Revolution, Laurens took his three sons to England to be educated. John, the oldest, studied law. However, he returned to America in 1776 and served in the Revolution.

Meanwhile, in South Carolina, Laurens, who initially hoped for reconciliation with England, was elected to the Provincial Congress on January 9, 1775. As he became convinced of the need for independence, he became the President of the Committee of Safety and presided over the Congress from June until March 1776. He was then appointed the Vice President of South Carolina through June 27, 1777.

Laurens was elected to the Continental Congress on January 10, 1777, serving until 1780. From November 1, 1777, until December 9, 1778, he was the President of Congress, succeeding John Hancock. During this time, he oversaw the debate and creation of the Articles of Confederation while the Congress was in York, Pennsylvania. Laurens signed the document as President. He then led the transfer of the Congress back to Philadelphia on July 2, 1778.

Congress named Laurens the Minister to the Hague (Netherlands) in the fall of 1779. In early 1780, he traveled to Amsterdam and gained Dutch support for the colonies. However, on his return trip, while aboard the packet *Mercury* off the coast of Newfoundland, Laurens was captured by the HMS *Vestal*. Laurens tossed his dispatches in the water, but they were recovered. Among them was the draft of a treaty with the Dutch that prompted the British to declare war on the Dutch Republic, triggering the Fourth Anglo-Dutch War. Laurens, charged with treason, was examined by British officials. Some of the interrogation by Lord Hillsborough was published in newspapers in England and the colonies:

> "Is your name Henry Laurens?"
> "It is."
> "Are you the same Henry Laurens who was the President of the Congress in America?"
> "I am."
> "We are ordered by the King and Council to examine you and have certain questions to propose."
> "Your Lordships may save yourselves the trouble of an examination, as I think it my place to answer no questions you may put."
> "Sir, we are directed to commit you [as a] prisoner to the Tower."
> "I am ready to attend."

Thus, former President Henry Laurens became the only American held prisoner in the Tower of London. Fortunately, his former business mentor, Richard Oswald, still thought fondly of him and lobbied for his release. This finally occurred on December 31, 1781, when he was exchanged for General Lord Cornwallis, who was captured at Yorktown. He came home to find his plantation home, Mepkin, had been burned by the British, and the family lived in an outbuilding while they recovered.

Tragically, Colonel John Laurens, Henry's eldest son, was killed in 1782 at the Battle of the Combahee River before the Treaty of Paris ended the war. Father and son had argued over the years about the evils of slavery. John had urged his father to free his slaves and had offered the 40 he was to inherit to the cause, but Laurens did not relent and never manumitted his slaves.

In 1783, Laurens was sent to Paris to assist in negotiating peace with Britain, whose principal negotiator was Richard Oswald. Laurens, though not a signer of the Treaty of Paris, helped to negotiate settlements for the Netherlands and Spain.

Following the Revolution, Laurens retired from public life, declining to continue service in the Continental Congress or the Constitutional Convention. However, he served briefly in the state convention in South Carolina in 1788 for the ratification of the US Constitution.

Laurens died from complications of gout on December 8, 1792, at Mepkin. Due to his fear of being accidentally buried alive, the family waited three days before proceeding with his funeral. Laurens' will ordered the following:

> I come to the disposal of my own person. I solemnly enjoin it on my son (Henry Jr.) as an indispensable duty, that as soon as he conveniently can after my decease, he cause my Body to be wrapped in twelve yards of tow cloth, and burnt until it be entirely and totally consumed. And then collecting my bones, deposit them where ever he shall think proper.

Laurens is believed to be the first Caucasian to be cremated in the United States. However, it did not go well. The pyre was built along the banks of the Cooper River, and his remains were burned as wished. Accounts vary, but due to the amount of fluid in the body, the liquid poured forth and extinguished most of the flames prematurely. Then, the head broke from the corpse, hair aflame, and rolled down the bank into reeds by the water. A slave was sent into the mud to perform the gruesome task of retrieving it. His remaining bones, ashes, and charred head were then buried in the family plot at Moncks Corner, now on the grounds of Mepkin Abbey.

Some in the press did not approve of Laurens' method of disposal. There was a sonnet by someone using the penname Amicus titled "Lines

Before George

The gravestone of Henry Laurens, who was cremated.

written on reading the singular manner in which Henry Laurens, Esq. ordered his corpse to be disposed of." It read:

> The Pagans oft their funeral piles have made,
> To offer victims, or consume their dead;
> But who in Christian lands, e'er built a fire
> To expatiate their crimes, or burn a Sire!
> Will Christian people dread the worms of earth,
> Since they expect to rise to second birth?
> When Jesus bids the grave its prey resign,
> In his blest likeness they may hope to shine.

The city and county of Laurens, South Carolina, are named for Laurens. The village of Laurens in New York is also named for him. Laurens County, Georgia, is named for his son John. Fort Laurens in

Henry Laurens (1724–1792)

Ohio was named for Henry by his friend, General Lachlan McIntosh. Historian C. James Taylor summarized Laurens as follows:

> In both his public and private life, Henry Laurens' commitment to duty and hard work were recognized and admired. Unfortunately, his impatience and criticism of individuals who did not meet his standards made him appear petty and inflexible. As the strongest political figure in South Carolina during the transition from provincial to state government, he worked to protect the rights of Loyalists and moderate the zeal of the radicals. In Congress, his constancy during the British occupation of Philadelphia and the trying exile at York may have been his most significant contribution to the national cause. The poor health he endured after confinement in the tower and the emotional shock of his son John's death in August 1782 robbed him of the vigor that had marked his career to that time.

Warning of the dangers near the grave of Henry Laurens.

John Jay
(1745–1829)

"The Diplomatic President"

Buried at John Jay Cemetery,
Rye, New York

**Continental Association • Secretary of Foreign Affairs
United States Supreme Court**

This accomplished founder served the young country in multiple positions during his long public career. He was elected to the first and second Continental Congress where, in the latter, he also presided as the President of Congress. During the Revolutionary War, he represented the United States in Spain. He followed that by joining the American team assigned to negotiate the Treaty of Paris with England, which ended the war. Under the Articles of Confederation, he ably filled the position of Secretary of Foreign Affairs. A vocal proponent of a strong national government, he was a co-author of the *Federalist Papers*, which set forth the arguments in favor of the ratification of the United States Constitution. President Washington chose him to be the first Chief Justice of the Supreme Court. While serving in that post, he negotiated the controversial Jay Treaty with Great Britain. He concluded his career as a two-term Governor of New York. His name was John Jay.

Jay was born on December 12, 1745, in New York City. His father, Peter Jay, was a wealthy merchant who traded in furs, timber, and other

John Jay (1745–1829)

John Jay

products. His mother was Mary Van Cortlandt, who could trace Dutch ancestry and whose father served in the New York Assembly and was twice elected mayor of New York during colonial times. The Jays had ten children, seven of which survived to adulthood. Three months after their son John was born, the Jays left New York City and settled in Rye, New York.

Jay was educated at home by his mother until he was eight years of age, when he was sent to continue his schooling under the guidance of an Anglican priest. In 1760, at the age of 14, he entered King's College (now Columbia). Among the friends he made at Columbia was Robert Livingston, a man who would later become one of Jay's staunch critics. After graduating, he studied the law and was admitted to the New York bar in 1768. He and Robert Livingston then agreed to work together as partners. At the time, partnerships among attorneys were rare, but Jay and Livingston believed by working together and utilizing their connections, they were likely to attract more clients. The partnership lasted two years, after which the pair, both feeling they were on a successful path, opened law practices of their own.

During this period, Jay found time for other pursuits besides handling his legal work. According to one of his biographers, Walter Stahr, in his work *John Jay Founding Father*, the young lawyer was a leading member of a group known as the "Social Club" and was the manager of a dancing assembly. Stahr surmises that it was at a dance where Jay met Sarah Livingston in 1772 or 1773. Livingston, the eldest daughter of New Jersey Governor William Livingston, was sixteen years at the time but known for her intelligence and beauty. One of Jay's friends and fellow founder, Gouverneur Morris wrote of her, "never was a creature so admired." Jay married Livingston in the parlor of her father's home on April 28, 1774. The couple would have six children, and Sarah Livingston would be a major support and influence on Jay throughout her life. In his work on Jay, Stahr describes Sarah as "an ardent American patriot, perhaps more vocal than her restrained husband."

As the newlyweds spent their honeymoon in New York's northern counties, there was political activity in New York City. In response to the punitive measures imposed on Boston as a result of the Boston Tea Party, New Yorkers had appointed a committee to "take into consideration the measures of Parliament relative to Boston." When Jay and his wife returned to the city in late May, Jay learned that he had been named to this committee. At the initial meeting of this group consisting of 51 men, Jay was appointed to a subcommittee of four assigned to prepare a response to a letter the New Yorkers had received from Boston. The subcommittee drafted a letter that called for a meeting of delegates from all the colonies to review the situation in Boston and determine how to protect "our common rights." In July, the committee of 51 appointed Jay and four others to represent New York at the Continental Congress.

On September 5, 1774, the delegates to the First Continental Congress met in Philadelphia. The early meetings generally took care of housekeeping items, such as choosing Charles Thomson to serve as their secretary. Early in their initial meetings, an express rider arrived and reported that there had been fighting between British troops and

John Jay (1745–1829)

Americans near Boston and that British cannons had begun firing at the city. The delegates viewed this report as an indication that a war with the mother country had started, and many were relieved to learn that the report was false. However, other delegates viewed the concern over the report as an indication that the colonies were ill-prepared to take up arms and that this issue needed to be addressed.

Congress then appointed a committee of 24, including Jay, to prepare a paper detailing the colonists' rights, their grievances with England, and proposals on addressing the problems. With both loyalists and those considered radicals like John Adams, the committee found it difficult to reach a consensus. Although Jay was generally considered a conservative, he sided with Adams during the committee debates. The problem of reaching an agreement was solved when Paul Revere arrived, carrying a copy of the Suffolk Resolves. The Resolves called on the people of Massachusetts to resist "the unparalleled usurpation of unconstitutional power" while at the same time affirming that King George was "our rightful sovereign." After a single day of debate, Congress unanimously approved the Resolves.

As a member of Congress, Jay also took part in the debates that led to the Continental Association. As detailed by Stahr, according to notes taken by John Adams, Jay took the position that "negotiation, suspension of commerce, and war are the only three things. War is by general consent to be waived at present. I am for negotiation and suspension of commerce." Thus, on October 20, 1774, Congress formed the Continental Association effective December 1, 1774, that prohibited both imports and exports with Great Britain, Ireland, and the British West Indies. Jay became one of the signers of the Association.

In April of 1775, Jay was once again one of the New Yorkers elected to represent his state at the Second Continental Congress. As relations between the colonies and England grew worse, he remained as one of the members of Congress who hoped to avoid war and reconcile with Great Britain. In May of 1776, Jay left Congress to spend time with his wife, who was ill, and with his father, who also suffered from poor health. During this time, he served as a member of New York's Provincial Congress. As a result, Jay was not in Philadelphia when Congress voted to approve the Declaration of Independence. Some question whether he would have supported the measure, but John Adams certainly was not one of them. On July 4, 1823, In Quincy, Massachusetts, Adams rose to offer a toast and said to, "the excellent President, Governor, Ambassador and Chief Justice, John Jay, whose name was not subscribed to the Declaration of Independence, as it ought to have been, for he was one of its ablest and faithful supporters."

When Adams called Jay an excellent president, he referred to his service as the President of Congress. Jay was elected to that position in the summer of 1778. During his tenure, Congress had problems due to a high turnover of delegates and their frequent absences. Nevertheless, Jay held this post for ten months, and during this period, he composed more than 500 letters on behalf of Congress. He also had the responsibility to meet with and entertain representatives from foreign countries.

Jay's time as President of Congress was a difficult one for him. According to his biographer, it has been called the "year of division." That same historian concludes that his greatest contribution may have been preventing a quarrelsome Congress from descending into chaos. Jay himself grew in the role. Through correspondence and by supporting the Commander in Chief, he had solidified a friendship with George Washington. In addition, his frustrations turned his thoughts to creating a strong national government. Finally, his knowledge about the views of the major members of Congress would aid him in the tasks he now undertook. First as his country's representative in Spain and then in Paris when he joined the American team whose job was to negotiate a peace treaty with England.

Jay and his wife Sarah set sail for Spain in late October 1779. Congress had given Jay the task of seeking recognition of the United States and hopefully an alliance against England as well as financial support from Spain for the new nation. Knowing he had little to offer the European country in return, he wrote Washington noting that the goals of his mission, "however just, will not be easily attained, and therefore its success will be precarious and probably partial." As it turned out, even these limited hopes proved to be unattainable. Spain refused to receive Jay as the Minister of the United States and declined to recognize

American independence because of concerns that such recognition could ignite similar revolutions in their colonies. Nevertheless, Jay successfully obtained a $170,000 loan that the United States government pledged to repay. After this very modest success, he left Spain in May of 1782 and headed to Paris to join in the negotiations with England to end the Revolutionary War.

The American negotiating team included Jay, Benjamin Franklin, John Adams, and Henry Laurens. However, only Jay and Franklin were present in Paris; the other Americans would join them later. David Hartley and Richard Oswald represented England. Congress had directed the American team to keep the French government informed about the progress of the talks. Jay wrote a letter protesting this directive because he believed the Americans could achieve better terms without French involvement. Congress reversed their decision, and a treaty was negotiated with favorable terms for the United States. The Treaty of Paris was signed on September 3, 1783, and included British recognition of the United States as an independent nation and established boundaries that allowed the new country to expand westward. According to Arthur G. Sharp in his work, *Not Your Father's Founders,* the most surprised countries on hearing of the accord were France and Spain. John Adams gave Jay the bulk of the credit for the treaty saying he was "of more importance than any of the rest of us." Adams also noted that the French had bestowed on him the title of 'le Washington of the negotiation.' He called the description a flattering compliment to which he had not a right, saying it "belongs to Mr. Jay."

When Jay returned to New York in July of 1784, he learned that Congress had elected him to the post of Secretary of Foreign Affairs. As detailed by the historian Joseph Ellis in his book *The Quartet,* Jay set certain conditions for accepting the post. He required that he be free to appoint his staff, that he could speak as a representative of the confederation as a collective and (in the words of Ellis) "a rather audacious demand that the Congress move from its current location in Trenton to New York to facilitate his family obligations. It is a measure of Jay's prestige and the delegates' desperation that all the conditions he proposed were found acceptable."

Before George

In his new post, Jay sought to establish a strong American foreign policy. He prioritized establishing a stable American currency and paying off the country's Revolutionary War debt. He also worked to secure the recognition of the new nation by the established European powers. Jay also concerned himself with securing Newfoundland fishing rights and setting the country's borders under the best terms available at the time, and protecting American sailing ships from pirates. Unfortunately, his efforts were hampered by a Congress that was often absent or indecisive. Moreover, the country under the Articles of Confederation had neither an army nor a navy, so war may well have been disastrous. So, it may be said that his chief accomplishment when he left this post in 1789 was avoiding any such conflict.

When the Constitutional Convention was held in Philadelphia in 1787, Jay was blocked from joining the New York delegation by Governor George Clinton and his upstate supporters. By this time, Jay was known to be a proponent of a strong national government, which Clinton opposed. Jay had exhibited his preference for a strong executive branch as far back as 1777 when practically on his own he wrote the New York Constitution, which gave more authority to the executive than any other state constitution. As a result, the only member of the New York delegation who was a nationalist was Alexander Hamilton, who was certain to be outvoted by the other two New York delegates who opposed any changes to the Articles of Confederation.

After the convention produced the proposed Constitution, Jay took a leading role in supporting its ratification. He joined Hamilton and James Madison in writing *The Federalist Papers*. The papers were a series of 85 articles aimed at persuading reluctant New York state convention members to ratify the new Constitution. This would be a major task when New York chose its state delegates to consider the matter; only 19 of the 65 elected were known to favor ratification. Jay, of course, was one of them.

The convention met in Poughkeepsie, New York, and Jay proved to be a major force during the debates. Many of those opposed to the Constitution called for its approval only with amendments that a second Constitutional Convention would be required to consider. Others supported ratification conditioned upon a right to secede from the union. A vote of 31 to 28 defeated the latter proposal.

Jay drafted a letter to address the question of amendments. The letter New York would send to the other states urged them to call another convention to consider proposed amendments. New York did propose amendments, but the state ratified the Constitution without making their adoption or consideration by a second convention a requirement. The vote to ratify was also a close one, 30 to 27. Jay proved successful in using both the carrot and the stick to sway those opposed to his side. The carrot being support for consideration of amendments to the Constitution and the stick being that New York City would secede and form its state if New York failed to ratify. Indeed, Jay's letter may well have been the driving force that resulted in New York joining the Union without conditions.

Once the Constitution had been ratified, it was obvious that George Washington would be the first president. When the president went about assembling his cabinet, he offered Jay the Secretary of State position. This post would have continued his role as Secretary of Foreign Affairs, and he declined the offer instead of accepting a position Washington called "the keystone of our political fabric" Chief Justice of the United States. Washington nominated Jay to the position on the same day he signed the Judiciary Act of 1789, which created the post. Two days later, Jay was unanimously confirmed by the United States Senate. The Jay court's main role was establishing the rules and procedures the court would follow. Jay himself did establish a precedent for the Supreme Court in 1790 when the Treasury Secretary and his old friend Alexander Hamilton wrote to the Chief Justice asking that the Court endorse legislation allowing the federal government to assume state debts. Jay responded that the Court could not endorse legislation, only rule on the constitutionality of cases brought before it. Jay's response predated Chief Justice Marshall's court ruling in the landmark case *Marbury v. Madison* by more than a decade.

In 1792 The Federalist Party nominated Jay as its candidate for Governor of New York. Jay received more votes than his opponent George Clinton, but his majority was challenged based on vote technicalities in three counties that had delivered Jay his victory. Clinton supporters controlled the State legislature and the state courts, and as a result, enough Jay votes were disqualified to award Clinton the victory.

By the year 1794, the young United States of America was on the verge of another war with England. The former mother country blocked American exports, had failed to leave forts in the northern United States as called for by the Treaty of Paris, and seized American ships and supplies headed for France and impressing American sailors. President Washington gave Jay the task of negotiating a settlement with the English. In Jay's view, his country was totally unprepared for war. He negotiated what came to be known as the Jay Treaty, which ended British control of the northwestern forts but failed to address the country's concern relative to shipping rights and impressment. The emerging political party led by Thomas Jefferson, known as the Democratic-Republicans, denounced the treaty. In the House, James Madison and in the Senate, Aaron Burr, made speeches condemning it. The opposition to the treaty allowed Jay to joke that he could if he wished, make his way from one end of the country to the other by the light of his burning effigies.

Nevertheless, president Washington stood by the treaty, approved by the Senate 20-10, receiving exactly the two-thirds majority required for its adoption. In August of 1795, Washington signed the treaty, and given the fact that while attacking Jay could be done easily, the same was not true when it came to Washington. As a result, the criticisms of the treaty became more moderate in tone. In Jay's view, he had achieved his primary objective, avoiding a war the United States was ill-prepared to fight.

Having been defeated in a disputed election for Governor of New York in 1792, Jay was the obvious Federalist choice for that office in 1795. In May of that year, he was elected Governor, and he resigned as Chief Justice on June 29, 1795. He served as New York's Governor until 1801. His accomplishments as Governor included reforming the prison system, limiting the death penalty and abolishing flogging, constructing canals, and signing a bill that would gradually end slavery in the state.

Despite the measures he took as Governor and the fact that he was a founder of the New York Manumission Society, Jay's record of slavery is mixed. As late as the 1810 census, he is recorded as owning a slave. He had over the years continued to purchase enslaved people and grant

John Jay's grave.

their freedom once he believed their work to "have afforded a reasonable retribution." Yet in the close 1792 election for Governor, his views on slavery cost him votes in upstate New York Dutch areas where slavery was very much practiced. Then in 1794, when he negotiated the Jay Treaty, he angered many southern Americans when he abandoned the demand for compensation for slaves who had been freed and transported to other areas by the British after the Revolution.

In 1801 Jay declined the Federalist nomination to run for another term as Governor. That same year President John Adams nominated Jay, and the Senate confirmed him to return to the Supreme Court as Chief Justice. But, again, Jay declined to serve, opting to retire from public life. Adam's then nominated John Marshall to the post and he became the man who shaped the modern Court and one of the most significant judges in the history of this country.

Jay retired to his farm in Westchester County, New York. His wife Sarah passed away shortly after that. Jay continued to enjoy good health, and with one very notable exception, he stayed out of the political arena. In 1819 he wrote a letter condemning Missouri's bid to enter the union as a slave state. He wrote that slavery "ought not to be introduced nor permitted in any of the new states."

On the evening of May 14, 1829, Jay suffered what probably was a stroke. He passed away three days later and was laid to rest per his wishes in what is known as the John Jay Cemetery in Rye, New York, only open to the public once a year. This is also the only Founder's cemetery protected by barbed wire.

For many years Jay was somewhat of a forgotten founder. Many people had heard of him, but few were aware of the depth of his accomplishments and contributions to the establishment of the United States of America. As the historian, Joseph Ellis has stated, "We can argue about who should be on the top of the list of most important founders until the cows come home, but it's clear he (Jay) should be part of the list."

Fencing with barbed wire protects the Jay Cemetery.

Samuel Huntington
(1731–1796)

"First President of the Confederation"

Buried at Colonial Cemetery (aka Old Norwichtown Cemetery),
Norwich, Connecticut

Articles of Confederation • Declaration of Independence

This founder happened to be the President of Congress on March 1, 1781, when the Articles of Confederation officially went into effect. The Articles essentially brought the individual colonies together and created the United States of America. It is because of his position in the Congress at the time that some point to this founder as the first president. Whether one agrees with that view is not important. The man can and should be remembered for his efforts on behalf and his contributions to the young country. Known for his great dignity and exceptional gentleness, he was described by those who knew him as "a sensible, candid and worthy man." He was among those who risked all by affixing his signature to the Declaration of Independence. His name was Samuel Huntington.

Huntington was born on July 16, 1731, in what is now Scotland, Connecticut. He was the firstborn of Nathaniel and Mehetabel Huntington's ten children. Since he was the oldest of ten children, he was expected to work the family farm. As a result, according to multiple sources, he never received any formal education. However, one researcher has written that Huntington graduated from Yale College in 1755.

Before George

Samuel Huntington

Considering his later success, this is entirely possible. When he reached the age of 16, he apprenticed with a barrel maker while at the same time continuing to assist his father with the farm. He somehow found the time to educate himself by borrowing books from local attorneys and his future father in law, the Reverend Ebenezer Devotion. It appears possible that the studies he undertook on his own could have prepared him for Yale. What is not in dispute is fueled by his industry; he became a practicing attorney after being admitted to the Connecticut bar in 1754.

In 1761 Huntington married Martha Devotion, the daughter of the aforementioned Ebenezer. The couple did not have any children of their own, but when one of Huntington's brothers died, they adopted his two children. Huntington and his wife stayed together until she died in 1794. The couple's adopted son, Samuel Huntington, became the third governor of Ohio.

By the age of thirty, Huntington was one of the most important lawyers in Connecticut. In 1765 he was named the King's Attorney for the colony apposition, making him Connecticut's attorney general. When

Samuel Huntington (1731–1796)

Huntington first entered politics a year before being appointed as the King's Attorney, as a member of the Connecticut General Assembly, he held conservative views and was loyal to the king. However, as the British Parliament began imposing oppressive measures on the colonies, his position changed, and he became an outspoken critic of the crown and resigned his office. In 1775 he was chosen along with Roger Sherman and Oliver Walcott to represent Connecticut in the Continental Congress. All three members of the Connecticut delegation were ardent advocates of independence. As a member of Congress, he voted for American independence and signed the declaration that proclaimed the separation of the colonies from the British empire.

In terms of his congressional service, in 1846 the historian Robert T. Conrad wrote that Huntington "devoted his talents and time to the public service. His stern integrity, and inflexible patriotism, rendered him a prominent member, and attracted a large share of the current business of the house; as a member of numerous important committees, he acted with judgment and deliberation, and cheerfully and perseveringly dedicated his moments of leisure to the general benefit of the country."

Huntington was not known as a great orator, nor did he write much or very well. He earned the respect of his fellow delegates through his diligence and hard work. When John Jay left Congress to become minister to Spain, Huntington was elected to succeed him as president in 1779. On March 1, 1781, the Articles of Confederation were signed, which made the thirteen colonies the United States of America. Because Huntington was the President of Congress, some point to him as the first President of the United States.

Five months after the signing of the Articles, Huntington was forced to resign from Congress and return to Connecticut due to illness. Despite battling health issues for the rest of his days, he remained active in public affairs. He served as chief justice of the Connecticut Supreme Court and as lieutenant governor of the state before serving as the third governor of the Constitution State. He advocated for religious tolerance, the abolition of slavery, and the ratification of the United States Constitution under which George Washington served as the generally recognized first president of the country. Huntington presided over the state convention that gathered to debate ratification.

Tomb of Samuel Huntington.

In 1900 Susan Huntington wrote about her ancestor in the *Connecticut Magazine*:

> Among the phalanx of Patriots who fearlessly and unbrokenly resisted the menaces and efforts of the British government to prevent the Declaration of Independence, it is remarkable to observe the great proportion that arouse from the humble walks of life who by the vigour [*sic*] of their intellect, and unwearied fearlessness compensated the deficiencies of early education and enrolled themselves with honor and capacity among the champions of Colonial freedom. Such a man was Samuel Huntington . . . His extreme modesty and the fact that he left no descendants perhaps account for so little appreciation of the value of his services in these days of revival of interest in all things relating to the American Revolution.

Huntington was serving as governor when he died on January 5, 1796. He was laid to rest just 15 miles away from the place of his birth

Samuel Huntington (1731–1796)

in the Old Norwichtown Cemetery that is now known as the Colonial Cemetery. In 2003 the citizens of Norwich raised $31,000 and used the funds to exhume both Huntington and his wife. The tomb was restored, and the bodies of the founder and his wife were placed in new caskets and reinterred. There rests a man who went from being a barrel maker to a signer of the Declaration of Independence, to become, at least according to the people of Norwich, the first President of the United States.

Thomas McKean
(1735–1817)

"First Elected President of the Confederation"

Buried at Laurel Hill Cemetery,
Philadelphia, Pennsylvania

**Military • Declaration of Independence
Articles of Confederation**

This founder was known for his very brusque take-charge attitude that at times upset his fellow patriots. This may have contributed to the fact that while serving in the Stamp Act Congress, two other delegates challenged him to duels which he speedily accepted. Only the departure of one representative and the existence of cooler heads avoided the shedding of blood. His resume is lengthy and in addition to service in Congress included service in the military. He also served as Governor of Delaware and as Chief Justice of Pennsylvania at the same time. He would later attend the Pennsylvania convention that ratified the United States Constitution and serve as the Governor of that state. He also affixed his signature to both the Declaration of Independence and the Articles of Confederation. Some contend that he served as one of the first Presidents of the United States under those Articles. His name was Thomas McKean.

McKean was born on March 19, 1734, in New London Township located in Chester County, Pennsylvania. His parents were both Irish born Ulster-Scots who came to America from Ballymoney, County

Thomas McKean (1735–1817)

Thomas McKean

Antrim, Ireland. When McKean was 16 years of age, he traveled to New Castle, Delaware to study the law under one of his cousins. By 1756 he had been admitted to the bar in both Delaware and Pennsylvania. By the mid-1760s he was serving in the Delaware General Assembly and as a judge of the Court of Common Pleas. Delaware at the time had two political factions which were commonly referred to as the "Court Party" and the "Country Party." The former party urged reconciliation with England while the latter, of which McKean was a leading member, supported American independence.

In 1765, Mckean and Caesar Rodney represented Delaware at the Stamp Act Congress. McKean was an active member of this group and along with John Rutledge and Philip Livingston served on the committee that drafted the Declaration of Rights and Grievances. Timothy Ruggles, a delegate from Massachusetts who served as president of the body, refused to sign the Memorial. Ruggles also declined to state the reasons for his objection. McKean wouldn't let the matter drop and demanded that Ruggles explain himself. The Massachusetts delegate then explained that his conscience would not permit him to address complaints to the king. McKean responded with scorn twice bellowing out the word conscience in a sarcastic manner that Ruggles viewed as an insult. He challenged McKean to a duel which was immediately accepted. Early the next morning Ruggles returned to his home state, so no duel was fought. The Massachusetts legislature officially censured Ruggles for "a neglect of duty." Ruggles wasn't the only delegate at the gathering to draw McKean's ire. Robert Ogden, a representative from New Jersey, also challenged McKean to a meeting on the field of honor. McKean accepted this invitation but cooler heads in attendance interceded, and the quarrel was settled without a shot being fired.

McKean would marry twice and father eleven children. His first wife, Mary Borden, passed away in 1773. A year later he married Sarah Armitage and moved his family to Philadelphia. Despite his Pennsylvania residence he was elected to represent Delaware in the Continental Congress. As a member of Congress, McKean is remembered for the part he played in fellow delegate Caesar Rodney's midnight ride. On July 1, 1776, McKean concluded that another delegate from Delaware, George Read, intended to vote against declaring American independence. Rodney, who like McKean favored independence, was absent from Congress due to a severe illness. Realizing that Rodney's vote would be needed McKean sent a messenger to Rodney who had returned to his home in Dover, Delaware. The message urged his fellow delegate to return to Philadelphia at once. Rodney immediately mounted a horse and began the eighty-mile trip back to Congress. As McKean later remembered in a letter to one of Rodney's nephews, he met Rodney "at the State-house door in his boots and spurs as the members were assembling; after a friendly salutation (without a word on the business) we went into the Hall of Congress together, and found we were among the latest: proceedings immediately commenced, and after a few minutes the great question was put; when the vote for Delaware was called, your uncle arose and said: 'As I believe the voice of my constituents and of all the sensible & honest men is in favor of Independence & my own judgment concurs with them I vote for Independence." Read voted nay but by a margin of two to one Delaware favored independence.

McKean did not get to sign the Declaration of Independence with his fellow members of Congress. Soon after casting his vote he led a militia group to assist George Washington during the unsuccessful defense of New York City. As a result of this military duty, McKean is considered to be the last signer of the Declaration of Independence. McKean insisted that he signed the document sometime in 1776 though most historians believe he affixed his signature to the document between 1777 and 1781.

The war years weren't quiet ones for McKean. He had been placed on the English hit list and wrote in a letter to John Adams that "he was being hunted like a fox." When the British captured the rebel governor of Delaware, McKean assumed the post. At the same time he was serving quite capably as Chief Justice of Pennsylvania in a post he filled from 1777 until 1799. According to his biographer John Coleman, "only the historiographical difficultly of reviewing court records and other scattered documents prevents recognition that McKean, rather than John Marshall, did more than anyone else to establish an independent judiciary in the United States. As Chief Justice under a Pennsylvania constitution he considered flawed, he assumed it the right of the court to strike down legislative acts it deemed unconstitutional, preceding by ten years the U.S. Supreme Court's establishment of the doctrine of judicial review."

In October of 1776 the during what was viewed as a conservative reaction against independence, the Delaware General Assembly did not re-elect McKean to the newly declared nation's Congress. Within a year British occupation of the state changed public opinion, and McKean was returned to Congress in 1777. He would serve in this body until 1783. He helped draft the Articles of Confederation and voted for their adoption in 1781. That same year he was elected to the position of President of Congress. Though primarily a ceremonial position with little authority some have argued that McKean served as President of the United States.

Though he did not attend the Constitutional Convention, McKean took a leading role in securing Pennsylvania's ratification of the United States Constitution. He argued in favor of a strong executive and was a member of the state convention that voted to ratify the document.

Before George

The grave of Thomas McKean.

When American political parties came into being, he allied himself initially with the Federalists. By the mid-1790s he broke with that party because of disagreements with compromises that the administration in Philadelphia made with Great Britain. He became an outspoken Jeffersonian Republican.

In 1799 McKean was elected to the first of three terms he would serve as Governor of Pennsylvania. As Governor, he demanded that things be done his way. He removed his critics from government posts and rewarded his supporters with jobs. His administration was so stormy that he had to survive an impeachment attempt by his political foes in 1807. In this, he proved successful.

Thomas McKean (1735–1817)

McKean passed away in 1817 at the age of 83. He was initially laid to rest in the First Presbyterian Church Cemetery, but his remains were moved to Philadelphia's Laurel Hill Cemetery in 1843. In a letter to one of McKean's sons, John Adams described his fellow founder as "among the best tried and firmest pillars of the Revolution."

McKean County, Pennsylvania is named in his honor. There is also a McKean Street in Philadelphia. Both the University of Delaware and Penn State University have buildings named for him.

John Hanson
(1715–1783)

"President During Yorktown"

Buried at Addison Burial Ground,
Oxon Hill, Maryland

Articles of Confederation

John Hanson was a merchant and politician from Maryland who was a member of the Continental Congress. He signed the Articles of Confederation and was then elected the first President of Congress Assembled after their ratification.

John Hanson was born on April 3, 1715, at the plantation "Mulberry Grove" in Port Tobacco Parish, Charles County, Maryland, the son of Samuel Hanson (1685–1740), a planter, and his wife, Elizabeth (née Storey) Hanson (1688–1764). Samuel owned more than 1,000 acres and served in various political offices, including the Maryland General Assembly. Hanson's grandfather, also named John, was an indentured servant who came to Charles County, Maryland, circa 1661.

There is no record or mention of Hanson receiving formal schooling, so it is assumed by historians he was tutored privately, as was customary. He followed in his father's footsteps, managing the plantation. Circa 1744, Hanson married Jane Contee of a well-known Maryland family. She was only sixteen at the time, and the couple remained married for Hanson's entire life. The couple had nine children, five of whom lived to adulthood.

John Hanson (1715–1783)

John Hanson

Hanson's first political office was sheriff of Charles County in 1750. He then followed his father as the representative of Charles County in the Maryland General Assembly, serving for twelve years starting in 1757. During the 1760s, Hanson was a leading agitator against the Sugar Act of 1764 and the Stamp Act of 1765. In 1769, he signed the nonimportation resolution boycotting British imports in response to the Townshend Acts. At this time, Hanson resigned from the General Assembly, sold his Charles County properties, and moved to Frederick County, Maryland. There, he was elected deputy surveyor, sheriff, and county treasurer.

As tensions increased with Great Britain in 1774, Hanson became a leading patriot in Frederick County. He led the passage of a town resolution opposing the Boston Port Act and sent 200 pounds of his own money to support the citizens. The next year, he was a delegate to the Maryland Convention that replaced the General Assembly and was the Maryland Committee of Correspondence chairman. He signed the

Association of Freeman on July 26, 1775, hoping for reconciliation, but calling for military resistance to the enforcement of the Coercive Acts.

Hanson was also highly active in organizing the local military, recruiting and arming soldiers, paying them with his own funds. Frederick County sent the first southern troops to join George Washington. They were led by Michael Cresap and Thomas Price, arriving in Boston on August 9, 1775, after marching twenty-two days. Hanson's son, Lieutenant Peter Contee Hanson, was among them. He was mortally wounded at Fort Washington and died in November 1775.

In June 1776, Hanson and his Frederick County patriots urged Maryland's delegates in the Continental Congress to declare independence from Britain. Meanwhile, Hanson was busy "making gunlocks, storing powder, guarding prisoners, raising money and troops, dealing with Tories, and doing the myriad other tasks which went with being chairman of the committee of observation."

In 1777, Hanson was elected to the new Maryland House of Delegates, serving five annual terms. In December 1779, they named him a delegate to the Second Continental Congress. Hanson began serving in Philadelphia in June 1780, immediately becoming involved in various finance committees. At the time, the ratification of the Articles of Confederation was stalled in Maryland because of concerns about western land claims. After the other states agreed to relinquish their western claims that interfered with Maryland, Hanson and Daniel Carroll signed the Articles on March 1, 1781. At this point, the Articles were officially ratified at the national level and went into effect.

Since its inception, the Continental Congress had a presiding officer titled the President of Congress who oversaw the debates and deliberations. Eight men had played this part in the early days of our nation. With the signing of the Articles of Confederation, the new office of President of the Congress Assembled was created as the first presiding officer of the officially united colonies. At that moment, Samuel Huntington, the incumbent President of Congress, transitioned from the prior role to the new one, but his term was now exceeding a year. On July 9, 1781, Samuel Johnston was the first man elected to the new office, but he declined. Thomas McKean was next elected but served only

John Hanson (1715–1783)

a few months, resigning after the surrender at Yorktown. On November 5, 1781, Congress elected Hanson as President of Congress Assembled, succeeding Thomas McKean. The role involved moderating discussions, handling official correspondence, and signing documents. Hanson did not enjoy the role out of the gate and discussed resigning after one week, citing his health and family responsibilities. His colleagues urged him to remain due to the lack of a quorum necessary to choose a successor. Hanson carried out his duty through his entire one-year term, ending November 4, 1782.

During his term, Hanson welcomed George Washington back to Philadelphia following his victory at Yorktown. Washington presented Cornwallis's sword to Congress. He also lightened his administrative burden by creating executive departments to deal with the myriad of correspondence and contracts, including the Treasury Department, the first Secretary of War, and the first Foreign Affairs Department. He saw to the removal of all foreign troops from American lands, as well as their flags. He gained agreement on the eventual statehood of the Western Territories. Hanson was also responsible for establishing Thanksgiving Day as the fourth Thursday in November. Elias Boudinot succeeded Hanson on November 5, 1782, but he continued as a delegate in the Congress for one more term.

In 1783, Hanson retired from Congress and returned to his nephew's estate near Oxon Hill in Prince George's County, Maryland. Oddly, word circulated in the papers that he had died in May 1783, but he had not. Retractions followed,

> The account published in the Philadelphia papers, of the death of the Honorable John Hanson, Esq; late President of Congress, we have the pleasure of assuring the public is premature; that worthy patriot being now in perfect health.

However, Hanson did die later in the year, on November 22, 1783. He was entombed on the estate at Oxon Hill, now known as the Addison Burial Ground. Unfortunately, the exact location of his grave has been lost, and the precise location of his remains is unknown. There was substantial development in the area, and the grave may have been vandalized.

According to biographer Seymour Weyss Smith, the American Revolution had two primary leaders: George Washington over the military and John Hanson in politics. However, this biography has been criticized as lacking academic support.

Of Hanson's children, Jane Contee Hanson (1747–1781) married Philip Thomas (1747–1815); Peter Contee Hanson, as mentioned, died at Fort Washington; and Alexander Contee Hanson (1749–1806) was a notable essayist. Alexander's son, by the same name, was a newspaper editor and U.S. senator from Maryland from 1813 to 1819.

John Hanson is one of the two Marylanders honored with a statue in the National Statuary Hall Collection in Washington, D.C. However, some lawmakers have recently lobbied to replace it with Harriet Tubman.

In 1972, Hanson was honored with a U.S. postal card featuring his name and portrait. He was also featured on a postage stamp. Route 50 between Washington, D.C., and Annapolis is named the John Hanson Highway. Middle schools in Oxon Hill and Waldorf, Maryland, are named after him. At one time, there was a bank named in his honor.

Since the 1970s, April 14 is John Hanson Day in Maryland thanks to a measure sponsored by descendent John Hanson Briscoe, who served as Speaker of the Maryland House of Delegates. The Hanson Memorial Association was created in 2009 to erect the John Hanson National Memorial and educate the public about Hanson. The memorial includes a statue at the courthouse in Frederick, Maryland.

Elias Boudinot
(1740–1821)

"President During the Treaty of Paris"

Buried at Saint Mary's Episcopal Churchyard,
Burlington, New Jersey

Military • US Congress • Mint Director

Elias Boudinot was a deeply devout Christian, abolitionist, lawyer, statesman, and soldier who served under George Washington as an intelligence officer and commissary for prisoners of war. Boudinot served in the Continental Congress and was its president at the end of the Revolution. He later served as a member of the US House of Representatives and as the Director of the US Mint. In 1816, he founded the American Bible Society which has since distributed billions of Bibles worldwide. As a Congressman, he proposed a national day of Thanksgiving.

Boudinot was born on May 2, 1740, in Philadelphia, Pennsylvania, to Elias Boudinot III and his wife, Mary Catherine (née Williams) Boudinot. The elder Boudinot was a merchant and silversmith who was a neighbor and friend of Benjamin Franklin. Boudinot's paternal lineage was French Huguenot. His mother's ancestors were Welsh. The couple married in 1729 and had nine children, five of whom reached adulthood. Sister Annis became the first published female poet in the colonies. Brother Elisha later became Chief Justice of the New Jersey Supreme Court.

Boudinot was tutored in the classics at home and then studied law under Richard Stockton in Princeton, New Jersey, who had married his

Before George

Elias Boudinot

sister Annis. In 1760, Boudinot was admitted to the New Jersey bar and set up a prosperous law practice in Elizabeth, New Jersey. On April 21, 1762, he married Hannah Stockton, his brother-in-law's younger sister. The Boudinots had nine children, four of whom survived to adulthood. One daughter, Susan, later married William Bradford, who became the Chief Justice of Pennsylvania and US Attorney General in the Washington administration.

Boudinot largely avoided politics prior to the Revolution. In 1774, he joined the Essex County Committee of Correspondence and chaired the county's Committee of Safety. He was also elected to the Provincial Congress of New Jersey in 1775. During these early months, Boudinot held out for reconciliation with England, even after the first shots were fired at Lexington and Concord. At a meeting in New Brunswick in April 1776, he voted against Dr. John Witherspoon's call for New Jersey's independence, though he hoped the Continental Congress would address the matter. Wrote Boudinot later:

> There appeared a general Approbation of the Measure, and I strongly suspected a universal Acquiescence of both Committees & Audience in approving the doctor's scheme... I never felt myself in a more mortifying Situation... Two of the Committee had delayed the Question by speaking in favor of it, but no one had spoken in Opposition, till I arose and in a Speech of about half an Hour or better, stated my peculiar Situation and endeavored to show the Fallacy of the Doctor's Arguments.

As Congress declared independence, with his brother-in-law's signature, Boudinot assisted the Patriot cause. He promoted enlistments, loaned money for supplies, and was the aide-decamp to William Livingston of the New Jersey militia. He was also involved in spy activities monitoring the British during the occupation of New York City from Staten Island and Long Island.

Impressed with Boudinot's work with Livingston, George Washington appointed him the Commissary General for Prisoners on May 5, 1777. Congress's Board of War agreed, and Boudinot was commissioned as a colonel in the Continental Army, serving until July 1778. In this role, he was responsible for supplying the American prisoners held by the British. Boudinot was soon at odds with the Congress, who were unreasonable regarding prisoner exchanges with the British. Where General Howe had suggested simple officer for officer, soldier for soldier, citizen for citizen exchanges, the Congress demanded hard currency. This made Boudinot's job more difficult and risked the treatment of prisoners. On March 8, 1778, he was summoned to Philadelphia for a meeting with an oversight committee of Congress where he explained his position for the fair treatment of prisoners on both sides as both moral and ethical and reflective of the wishes of General Washington. Boudinot, who had been elected to the Congress months earlier and had not taken his seat, filed his report. He had used his own money to fund the supplies for the prisoners. Wrote Boudinot at the time:

> When I found every application to obtain hard money from Congress for the Cloathing of our Prisoners in vain, I waited on Genl Washington, and proposed my resignation, as my Character was at stake, having (on the promise of the Secret Committee to yield me

every necessary aid) pledged myself to the officers in Confinement that they should be regularly supplied with every necessary, but they now suffered more than ever. In much distress and with Tears in his Eyes, he assured me that if he was deserted by the Gentn of the Country, he should despair. He could not do everything ... He was Gen. Quarter Master and Commissary. Everything fell on him and he was unequal to the task. He gave me the most positive Engagement that if I would contrive any mode for their Support and Comfort he would confirm it as far as was in his Power—On this I told him, I knew of but one way and that was to borrow Money on my own private Security. He assured me that in Case I did, and was not reimbursed by Congress, he would go an equal share with me in the loss. I then formed the plan of obliging Genl. Burgoyne to pay hard money for the support of the British Prisoners whom we supplied with daily rations, and in the meantime proceeded to borrow money or take Goods in New York on my own Credit. Thus I furnished 300 officers with a handsome suit of Cloaths each, and 1100 Men with a plain suit, Found them Blanketts, Shirts etc. and added to their provisions found by the British a full half ration of Bread and Beef p[e]r. day for upwards of 15 Months. Part of this I supplied by sending wheat and flour to New York, and selling them for hard money, under leave from Genl Robertson. Sometime in the beginning of the year 1778, Congress recd from Genl Burgoyne nearly 40,000 Dollars in hard money. In the beginning of 1778, I was chosen a Member of Congress, but continued in the Army till June, when Genl. Washington, knowing that I was near thirty Thousand Dollars in advance for the Prisoners, urged me to go and take my Seat in Congress, where I might get some of the hard money recd from Genl[.] Burgoyne before it was all expended, for if it was once gone, I should be totally ruined. I accordingly left the Army and joined Congress on their return from York Town in Pennsylvania, after the British had evacuated the City of Philadelphia. [10]

In July, he resigned from the commissary role, as General Washington suggested, and took his seat in Congress as a delegate from New Jersey.

In this new role, he continued to advocate for the treatment of prisoners. Boudinot left the Congress in 1779. But was reelected in 1781 and served through 1784. He was involved in the debates over the Articles of Confederation and the peace treaty with Britain. On November 4, 1782, despite his difficulties in the past with the Congress over prisoners, Boudinot was elected the President of the Confederation Congress, succeeding John Hanson. During Boudinot's year in the role, he signed the peace treaty with Great Britain on April 15, 1783. In June 1783, he led Congress's move from Philadelphia to Princeton, where they met at Nassau Hall on the college campus.

Boudinot left Congress at the end of his term and returned to New Jersey to practice law. After the US Constitution was ratified, he ran for office in the House of Representatives and served in the First through Third Congresses (from 1789 to 1795). On September 25, 1789, the day after the House of Representatives voted to recommend the First Amendment of the newly drafted Constitution to the states for ratification, Congressman Boudinot proposed that the House and Senate jointly request President Washington to proclaim a day of thanksgiving for "the many signal favors of Almighty God." Said Boudinot:

> "I cannot think of letting the session pass over without offering an opportunity to all the citizens of the United States of joining, with one voice, in returning to Almighty God their sincere thanks for the many blessings he had poured down upon them."

President Washington officially declared the Thanksgiving Holiday on October 3, 1789, setting the first official date as November 26, 1789.

Boudinot refused to align with political parties and was one of only nine representatives who voted against the Eleventh Amendment of the Constitution, regarding jurisdictional standing in lawsuits.

Following the death of his son-in-law, William Bradford, in 1795, daughter Susan, now a widow, moved in with her parents and began editing her father's papers regarding the Revolutionary era. In October of that year, President Washington named Boudinot to succeed David Rittenhouse as the Director of the US Mint in Philadelphia. He kept this position until resigning in July 1805. When he, Hannah, and Susan moved to a new home in Burlington, New Jersey. Hannah died a few years after the move, leaving Boudinot a widower with his daughter.

In addition to numerous civic, religious, and educational causes, for nearly fifty years, Boudinot was a trustee for Princeton University. He also speculated on large tracts of land in Ohio, owning more of Green Township in what is now the western suburbs of Cincinnati. In response to Thomas Paine's deistic *The Age of Reason* (1794), Boudinot wrote, in 1801, the Christian response, *The Age of Revelation*. He was elected as a member of the American Antiquarian Society in 1814. In 1816, a devout Presbyterian, he founded the American Bible Society and served as its president for the rest of his life.

The grave of Elias Boudinot.

Boudinot was a philanthropist later in life, giving away his fortune to aid freed Blacks and Native Americans. He gave away his Ohio lands to the benefit of the American Board of Commissioners for Foreign Missions. He also sponsored students at the Board School for Indians in Connecticut. A Cherokee student named Gallegina Uwatie, aka Buck Watie, stayed with the Boudinots in Burlington on his way to school. The young man was so impressed with Boudinot that he asked permission to take his name. He was later known as Elias Boudinot and became the editor of the first newspaper in the nation published in Cherokee and English, the *Cherokee Phoenix*.

Boudinot died in Burlington, New Jersey, on October 24, 1821, at 81. He was laid to rest at St. Mary's Episcopal Church Cemetery in Burlington. He willed 13,000 acres to the city of Philadelphia for parks and other uses.

There are many honors for Elias Boudinot, beyond an avenue in Cincinnati. There are also streets in Philadelphia and Princeton, a lane in Franklin Township, New Jersey, and a Place in Elizabeth, New Jersey. Elias Boudinot Elementary School is in Burlington, New Jersey, and the Boudinot-Southard Farmstead is in Bernards Township, New Jersey. Princeton Library holds the Boudinot-Stockton papers and many other family possessions and portraits.

Thomas Mifflin
(1744–1800)

"President Who Accepted Washington's Retirement"

Buried at Trinity Lutheran Church,
Lancaster, Pennsylvania

**Military • Continental Association • U.S. Constitution
First Governor of Pennsylvania**

Thomas Mifflin is a Founding Father of our country whose contributions have gone unheralded and are largely forgotten. He risked his life for American independence and democracy. He spent almost his entire life in public service. He was expelled from his church for fighting the British, served as President of the Continental Congress, was a signer of the U.S. Constitution, and was Pennsylvania's first governor. Despite his many accomplishments and his contributions as a Founding Father, there is no monument that identifies his grave. There is a roadside historical marker saying he is interred somewhere on the grounds of Trinity Lutheran Church. It is uncertain where precisely he is buried. In addition, there is little mention of his many distinguished accomplishments during his long life of service to his country and his state. One internet site claims the grave was paved over for a parking lot. There is a marble slab in the wall of the church that states he was a signer of the Constitution.

Thomas Mifflin was born on January 10, 1744, in Philadelphia where his parents were prominent Quakers. He attended local schools and in

Thomas Mifflin (1744–1800)

Portrait of Thomas Mifflin, 1773, by John Singleton Copley.

1760, graduated from the College of Philadelphia (today known as the University of Pennsylvania). He went into business with a local merchant and in 1765, he formed a partnership in the import and export business with his younger brother.

Mifflin married a distant cousin, Sarah Morris, in 1771. That same year, he was elected city warden. In 1772, he began the first of four consecutive terms in the Colonial legislature. In the summer of 1774, Mifflin was elected by the legislature to the First Continental Congress. His work there spread his reputation across America and led to his election to the Second Continental Congress which convened in Philadelphia in the aftermath of the fighting at Lexington and Concord.

He played a major role in the creation of Philadelphia's militia and was commissioned as a major in May 1775. Despite his family being Quakers for generations, he was expelled from the church because military service violated the pacifist nature of the faith. In what had to be a difficult decision Mifflin viewed service to his country as more important than adherence to religious beliefs.

When Congress created the Continental Army in June 1775, Mifflin resigned from the militia to go on active duty with the regulars. George Washington, the Commander in Chief, selected Mifflin as one of his aides. Shortly after, Washington appointed him Quartermaster General of the Continental Army. His service as Quartermaster earned him a promotion to Brigadier General, but he longed for a field command and requested to be reassigned. He was transferred to the infantry and led a brigade of Pennsylvania continentals during the New York City campaign. He fought bravely in the battles of Long Island, Trenton, and Princeton, and was with Washington during the terrible winter at Valley Forge. Throughout this time his persuasive oratory convinced many men not to leave the military service. However, he was soon returned to the position of Quartermaster when no suitable replacement could be found for him. It was a move that left him bitterly disappointed.

In November 1776, General Mifflin was sent by Washington to Philadelphia to report to the Continental Congress on the critical condition of the army. The Continental Army was outgunned and outmanned and unable to make a stand in New Jersey to stop the advancing British march towards Philadelphia. It was a wise move by the Commander-in-Chief to send General Mifflin to rally Philadelphia, as Congress, in fear of losing the capital was preparing to take flight to Baltimore. When the Continental army was forced into Pennsylvania, the citizens of Philadelphia began to panic. Business was suspended, schools were closed, and roads leading from the city were crowded with refugees all fleeing the city.

At a town meeting, General Mifflin addressed the crowd and much of the Continental Congress. After listening to Mifflin, Congress formally appealed to the militia of Philadelphia and surrounding areas to join Washington's army. Mifflin organized and trained three regiments of militia and sent 1,500 men to Washington. He also orchestrated a re-supply of Washington's desperate troops once they reached Valley Forge. These were critical components needed by Washington to cross the Delaware and attack the British in Trenton. In recognition of his services, Congress commissioned Mifflin as a major-general and made him a member of the Board of War.

On the Board of War, General Mifflin joined a growing number of delegates and generals who shared the dissatisfaction of General Washington's conduct of the war. He sympathized with the views of General Horatio Gates and General Thomas Conway who blamed Washington for the losses of the Continental Army. In the fall of 1777, Horatio Gates, with the help of Benedict Arnold, defeated the British forces at Saratoga. Almost immediately, Washington's enemies, emboldened by the victory, sought his replacement with the "Hero of Saratoga" General Gates. General Conway organized an effort to have the Board of War establish Gates as the new Commander-in-Chief. This became known as "The Conway Cabal." When the effort failed, Mifflin submitted his resignation. Congress refused to accept it, but he was discharged from the Board of War.

In late 1778, while still on active duty, he won re-election to the State Legislature. In 1780, he was again elected to the Continental Congress and in 1783, the Continental Congress elected him as President of the Congress. He presided over the ratification of the Treaty of Paris, which

Plaque honoring Thomas Mifflin on the street-side of Trinity Lutheran Churchyard in Lancaster, Pennsylvania (photo by Joe Farrell).

ended the Revolution and ironically accepted Washington's formal resignation as Commander-in-Chief. In what many historians say was one of the most remarkable events of United States history George Washington was formally received by President Thomas Mifflin and Congress. At the pinnacle of his power and popularity, Washington resigned his commission as Commander-in-Chief to the President of the Continental Congress, a man who had once conspired to replace him.

Mifflin represented Pennsylvania at the United States Constitutional Convention and was a signer of it. He presided over the committee that wrote Pennsylvania's first constitution which established a bicameral legislature with a strong governor. He then ran for governor in 1790 and was elected as Pennsylvania's first governor by a margin of almost ten to one. He served three terms as governor until 1799.

Thomas Mifflin died on January 20, 1800, in Lancaster and was buried in the cemetery of Trinity Lutheran Church at state expense since his estate was too small to cover funeral costs. The cemetery no longer exists. Most of the bodies were moved in the 1840s to Woodward Hill Cemetery, but Mifflin's was not. There is a historical marker on South Duke Street that says, "here are interred the remains of Thomas Wharton, Jr. and Governor Thomas Mifflin."

Richard Henry Lee
(1732 – 1794)

"First President of the US Dollar"

Buried at Lee Family Plot,
"Burnt House Field" plantation, Coles Point, Virginia

**Continental Association • Declaration of Independence
Articles of Confederation**

Richard Henry Lee, the brother of Francis Lightfoot Lee and cousin of "Light Horse Harry" Lee, was a Continental Congressman who signed the Continental Association, Declaration of Independence, and Articles of Confederation. He was also the President of Congress (1784-1785). He is best known for proposing the Lee Resolution, the motion in the Continental Congress calling for independence from Great Britain. He was also a United States Senator from (1789-1792).

Lee was born January 26, 1732, at "Machadoc," later known as "Burnt House Field," in Hague, Westmoreland County, Virginia. He was the fifth son, and one of eleven children, of Thomas Lee, a planter in Virginia, and his wife Hannah Harrison (née Ludwell) Lee. Thomas Lee, the president of the Virginia Colonial Council, was a leading Virginia planter with over 30,000 acres of land prior to his death in 1750. After the completion of "Stratford Hall," in Westmoreland County, Virginia, a few years later, the family moved there.

Richard was taught by private tutors at "Stratford Hall." He was then sent to England to study at Wakefield Academy in Yorkshire. When his

Before George

Portrait of Richard Henry Lee by Charles Willson Peale.

parents died in 1750, his oldest brother, Phillip Lee, urged him to return home, but he refused, instead going on a tour of mainland Europe.

Richard returned to the colonies in 1753 and continued his studies. In 1755, during the French and Indian War, he was named the head of a volunteer militia serving under General Edward Braddock. Fortunately for Lee, Braddock did not utilize his unit and he saw no action nor did he play a role in the fateful Braddock Expedition. Lee married Anne Aylett in December 1757, and settled at his plantation, "Chantilly-on-the-Potomac," near "Stratford Hall." Richard and Anne had four children—two sons and two daughters. The following year, while hunting, Lee's gun exploded in his hands, taking all but one finger on his left hand. For the remainder of his life, Lee wore a glove to cover up the wound. Later that same year, Anne Lee died of pleurisy.

In 1764, Lee was named to a committee by the House of Burgesses to send a message to the king calling for an end to harmful economic measures being enacted against the colonies. In February 1766, Lee was one of the leading figures behind the establishment of the Westmoreland Association. One surviving draft of that document in Lee's hand stated,

> ... the Birthright privilege of every British subject (and of the people of Virginia as being such) founded on Reason, Law, and Compact; that he cannot be legally tried but by his peers; and that he cannot be taxed, but by the consent of a Parliament, in which he is represented by persons chosen by the people. The Stamp Act does absolutely direct the property of the people to be taken from them without their consent.

In 1767, Lee was a justice of the peace in Westmoreland County. The following year, he was elected to the Virginia House of Burgesses, taking the seat of his brother Philip. He served until 1775 along with his brothers Thomas Ludwell Lee and Francis Lightfoot Lee. In this body, he railed against slavery wanting to tax it into oblivion. He believed slaves were entitled to equal freedom and liberty. Such views put him at odds with most of the men in that body. In 1769, Lee married Anne Gaskins

"Burnt House Field," Lee Family Estate, in Coles Point, Virginia (photo by Lawrence Knorr).

Packard, a widow, and together the couple would have three daughters and two sons.

In 1773, Richard Lee was a member of the Virginia Committee of Correspondence along with Peyton Randolph, Robert Carter Nicholas, Richard Bland, Benjamin Harrison, Edmund Pendleton, Patrick Henry, Dudley Digges, Dabney Carr, Archibald Cary, and Thomas Jefferson. The following year, Lee was elected to the Continental Congress where he served until May 1779. During this time, Lee was a signer of the Continental Association, the Declaration of Independence, and the Articles of Confederation.

Regarding independence, Lee was an early and ardent proponent. Following Lexington and Concord, he was still in the minority, but as time went by, more and more delegates joined him. On June 7, 1776, Lee put forth a motion for independence,

> Resolved: That these United Colonies are, and of right ought to be, free and independent States, that they are absolved from all allegiance to the British Crown, and that all political connection between them and the State of Great Britain is, and ought to be, totally dissolved.

There was rancorous opposition to the motion, so much so that the President of Congress, John Hancock, had to table it to avoid a fight. Meanwhile, the Committee of Five including Thomas Jefferson, Ben Franklin, John Adams, Roger Sherman, and Robert Livingston set about drafting a formal declaration. Though absent on July 4th, Richard and his brother Francis returned in August to sign the document, being the only brothers to do so.

Soon after, Lee was accused by John Hancock and Robert Morris of conspiring with John and Samuel Adams to remove Washington as commander of the Continental Army. At this time his brother Arthur Lee was serving as a diplomat to France along with Benjamin Franklin and Silas Deane. Arthur informed Richard that Deane was using the position for his own personal gain. Richard took to the floor of the Congress and denounced Deane and moved to recall him from Paris. Deane did so and defended himself before Congress, causing a rift in the body. This forced Henry Laurens to resign as the President of Congress. In retaliation, Deane accused the entire Lee family of corruption. Lee's friend, John Adams, wrote to Samuel Cooper in February 1779 a defense of the Lee family,

> The complaint against the family of Lees is a very extraordinary thing indeed. I am no idolater of that family or any other, but I believe their greatest fault is having more men of merit in it than any other family; and if that family fails the American cause, or grows unpopular among their fellow-citizens, I know not what family or what person will stand the test.

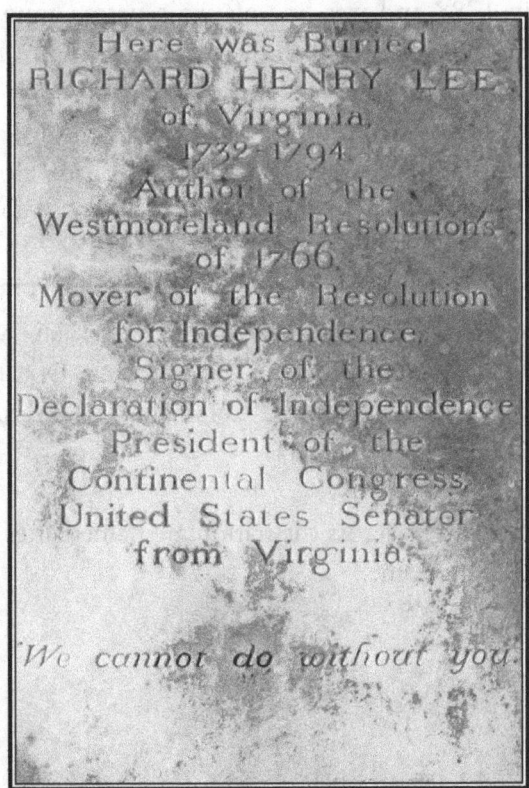

Detail from Richard Henry Lee's gravestone (photo by Lawrence Knorr).

Before George

Lee soon resigned from his seat in the Congress and returned to Virginia where he continued to serve in the state House of Delegates and as a colonel in the Westmoreland militia.

In 1784, Colonel Arthur Campbell wrote to encourage Lee to reconsider service in the Continental Congress. He did so and was elected in June 1784. At that point, Thomas Mifflin resigned as President of Congress and the position was vacant for several months. In November, Lee agreed to take the position and held it until November 1785 when he was succeeded by John Hancock. During his tenure, the U.S. dollar was established as the currency of the land, tied to the Spanish dollar (piece of eight). The Congress also unsuccessfully worked to sell western lands to cover the war debts.

Lee was a delegate to the Virginia convention to ratify the U.S. Constitution in 1788 and was one of two senators appointed to serve in the first Congress. He did so from March 1789 until he resigned in October 1792 as his health was beginning to fail.

Richard Henry Lee died on June 19, 1794, at the age of 62. Lee was buried at the Lee family estate's graveyard at "Burnt House Field," in Coles Point, Virginia. His gravestone reads,

> Here was buried Richard Henry Lee, of Virginia, 1732–1794. Author of the Westmoreland Resolutions of 1766. Mover of the Resolution for Independence. Signer of the Declaration of Independence. President of the Continental Congress. United States Senator from Virginia.

Many public schools across the nation are named after Lee. In 1941, a liberty ship bore his name.

Nathaniel Gorham
(1738–1796)

"President at Shay's Rebellion"

Buried at Phipps Street Cemetery,
Charlestown, Massachusetts

United States Constitution

Nathaniel Gorham was born in Charlestown, Boston, Massachusetts, on May 27, 1738. He was the son of Captain Nathaniel Gorham, a packet boat operator (a packet boat was a regularly scheduled service carrying freight and passengers), and his wife Mary Soley. His third great grandfather, John Howland, came to America on the *Mayflower* and signed the Mayflower Compact.

He received little formal education but was apprenticed at 15 to Nathaniel Coffin, a merchant in New London, Connecticut. He left Coffin's employ in 1759 and returned to Charlestown and established his own small business there, which quickly succeeded. Four years later, in 1763, he married Rebecca Call, and they had nine children together.

Gorham began his political career as a public notary but was soon elected to the colonial legislature (1771 to 1775), where he emerged as a staunch Patriot. During the Revolution, he displayed an exceptional talent for administrating that proved crucial to his state's wartime government. He was selected to serve on the Massachusetts Board of War, which organized Massachusetts' military logistics and manpower (1778–1781). In 1779 he was a delegate to Massachusetts' first constitutional convention. He represented his community in both the upper and lower houses of the new state legislature, serving several times as the lower house speaker.

Before George

Nathaniel Gorham

Gorham served as a delegate to the Continental Congress from 1782-83 and 1785-87 and served as its president after the resignation of John Hancock in June 1786. He served as president until November of that year.

In 1786, Gorham was involved in a very controversial matter that became known as the Prussian Scheme. Shay's Rebellion in western Massachusetts convinced many Americans that a stronger, centralized national government was necessary. The shortcomings of the Articles of Confederation were fanning the fears of anarchy. When Massachusetts debtors took up arms, refused to pay their debts, and closed the courts, Gorham predicted worse would follow.

These types of disturbances fueled the movement for convening a convention to modify the Articles of Confederation. Getting consensus to modify the Articles took some time. When the delegates convened in Philadelphia in May 1787, there were widely circulated rumors that the meeting was to offer to enthrone Prince Frederick of Prussia as king of the United States. So intense were the rumors that the convention issued a public denial that any proposal for reestablishing monarchy was being considered. The reason for these rumors was that Gorham, while President of the Continental Congress, wrote to Prince Henry, the younger brother of the Prussian King Frederick the Great, offering to make him king of the United States. Henry's response, found more than a century later, proved what many had assumed was a legend was to decline. He reportedly believed that the American public would not be likely to submit to a king. A letter addressed to Baron von Steuben, dated a few months before the Constitutional Convention, was discovered in the Prussian archives in the early 1900s. It refers to the offer and his refusal. Von Steuben, who was living in New York, was involved in the proposal. Some have attributed the natural-born citizen clause in the US Constitution as an attempt by the Philadelphia Convention to end the persistence of rumors of European royalty being invited to assume a hypothetical US throne.

Gorham was elected as a Massachusetts delegate to the Constitutional Convention in 1787. He played an influential part, frequently speaking, sitting on the Committee of Detail, and serving as chairman of the Committee of the Whole. He pushed for a central government strong enough to protect interstate commerce, promote international trade, and regulate the use of paper money. He favored long presidential and senatorial terms and the appointment of federal judges by the executive. He also wanted a consolidation of military authority through control of the militia by the central government.

To gain support for these things, he was willing to accept southern demands about slavery. Gorham was pessimistic about the future of his state and country. He believed, in the aftermath of Shay's Rebellion, that Massachusetts would divide between east and west over the constitution question and that the country would divide into several independent nations within 150 years.

He signed the Constitution and was a crucial participant in Massachusetts' struggle for ratification. Ratification was won only when

Before George

Gorham and other Federalists proposed possible amendments to the constitution to attract moderates. The final vote was 187 to 168.

Gorham did not serve in the new government he had helped create. In 1788 he and a friend Oliver Phelps bought 2,600,000 acres in western New York. The deal was a disaster and ruined him financially. By 1790 the two men were bankrupt, which led to a fall from the heights of Boston society and political esteem.

Gorham died in Charlestown, Massachusetts, on January 11, 1796, at the age of 58. He is buried in the Phipps Street Cemetery in Charlestown. Gorham Street in Madison, Wisconsin, and Gorham, New York are named in his honor.

The overgrown grave of Nathaniel Gorham.

Arthur St. Clair
(1737–1818)

"First President of Westward Expansion"

Buried at Saint Clair Park Path,
Greensburg, Pennsylvania

Military • First Governor of Northwest Territory

Arthur St. Clair, originally from Thurso, Scotland, was a political and military leader during the American Revolution and the first governor of the Northwest Territory in 1788 that later became Ohio, Indiana, Illinois, Michigan, and parts of Wisconsin and Minnesota.

St. Clair was a delegate to the Continental Congress who became its second to last President. He was also a major general in the Continental Army before losing his command following a retreat from Fort Ticonderoga. Later, in 1791, he was in command when American forces experienced their worst defeat by the Native Americans.

Historian Joseph J. Thompson called him "one of the most unique figures in American history... the handsome, polished, accomplished, profound St. Clair. The appearance and conduct of the men we have been considering were influenced by their rugged and rustic surroundings, but St. Clair was the product of culture and fashion."

Arthur St. Clair was born in Thurso, county of Caithness, Scotland in the 1730s. Some have estimated his birth year as 1734, but subsequent research points to March 23, 1736, as a reasonable date, which is 1737 on the modern calendar. The names of his parents are unknown, though

Before George

Arthur St. Clair

one biographer states they were "probably" William Sinclair, a merchant, and Elizabeth (née Balfour or Hamilton).

It is believed St. Clair attended the University of Edinburgh for a time but then left to study anatomy with Dr. William Hunter, a leading Scottish physician, around 1756. Soon after, he quit and purchased a commission in the British army as an ensign and served in North America during the French and Indian War.

During the war, he served under General Jeffrey Amherst at the capture of Louisburg, Nova Scotia in July 1758. The following spring, he was promoted to lieutenant and served under General James Wolfe at the Battle of the Plains of Abraham resulting in the capture of Quebec City.

After the battle, St. Clair went on leave in Boston where he met his future wife, Phoebe Bayard, the niece of Governor James Bowdoin of Massachusetts colony. St. Clair married her, resigned his commission, and decided to settle in the Ligonier Valley near modern-day Pittsburgh, Pennsylvania using funds from his father-in-law. There he invested in mills and took a position as a surveyor, becoming the largest landowner in the region. Despite not being a lawyer, he was named a local justice and in a 1774 almanac was listed as a prothonotary in Bedford and Westmoreland Counties.

St. Clair was a proponent of Pennsylvania in its disputes with Virginia regarding the Ohio Country and Fort Pitt area. St. Clair worked with the natives in the area to promote the fur trade rather than see them give up their lands to the Virginians. Lord Dunmore's War ultimately settled the boundaries between the settlers and the natives at the Ohio River. St. Clair's actions likely spared the settlers in the Fort Pitt area from native vengeance.

At the outset of the American Revolution, St. Clair was a supporter of the patriot cause. He served on his local Committee of Safety and was the secretary to the representatives from the Continental Congress who negotiated with the Indians of the Ohio Country. In 1775, the Congress appointed him as a colonel in the 3rd Pennsylvania Regiment of the Continental Army and he participated in the attack on Canada at the Battle of Trois-Rivières. Afterward, he was appointed to brigadier general and in August 1776 was sent by Washington to organize the New Jersey militia. During the winter of 1776-77, he was with Washington at the battles of Trenton and Princeton. He crossed the Delaware River with Washington on the night of December 25-26, 1776, and many biographers credit him with the strategy that led to the capture of Princeton. He was promoted to major general in February 1777.

In the spring of 1777, St. Clair was assigned to command Fort Ticonderoga in New York. When the British invaded, knowing he could not hold the fort without heavy casualties, St. Clair abandoned the fort and retreated. George Washington was disappointed he left without a fight. A subsequent court-martial headed by General Benjamin Lincoln, however, found St. Clair innocent of all charges. Despite his exoneration, St. Clair was not given significant commands for the remainder of the war though he was an aide-de-camp to General Washington, who retained a high opinion of him. St. Clair was at Cornwallis's surrender at Yorktown.

After the Revolution, St. Clair was elected to the Continental Congress, serving from November 2, 1785, to November 28, 1787. During his last year in Congress, St. Clair was elected President of

Congress, succeeding Nathaniel Gorham, on February 2, 1787, amid Shay's Rebellion. After the rebellion was put down, the Congress passed the Northwest Ordinance, creating the Northwest Territory (comprising modern-day Ohio, Indiana, Illinois, Michigan, most of Wisconsin, and eastern Minnesota), and assigned St. Clair as the governor. His presidency ended on October 29, 1787, when he took over his new duties.

St. Clair named Cincinnati, Ohio, after the Society of Cincinnati, and made his headquarters there. He formulated Maxwell's Code, named after its printer, as the first written laws in the territory. In 1789, he convinced certain Indians in the area to give up their land claims by signing the Treaty of Fort Harmar. Several chiefs had refused to participate or sign the treaty triggering the Northwest Indian War or Little Turtle's War. St. Clair, proceeded to build forts in western Ohio. He sent General Josiah Harmar and 1500 troops to suppress the Indians, ordering them to destroy the village of the Miami at present-day Fort Wayne, Indiana. Shawnee chief Blue Jacket and Miami chief Little Turtle defeated Harmar's men in October 1790 in what is known as Harmar's Defeat. Harmar retreated to Fort Washington, present-day Cincinnati, and St. Clair then took up command personally.

On March 21, 1791, Secretary of War Henry Knox ordered St. Clair to establish a strong and permanent military presence in the region. Congress commissioned St. Clair to lead two 300-man regiments of regular troops and 1400 ill-trained militiamen to move against the main Miami town, Kekionga.

St. Clair and his men left Fort Washington on September 17. The men marched twenty miles in two days and then built Fort Hamilton. They then advanced forty-five miles northward, where they erected Fort Jefferson. Leading primarily untrained militiamen, St. Clair faced problems with desertion from the beginning of his campaign. Although it was still early fall, his men faced cold temperatures, rain, and snowfall. Due to the scarcity of supplies, many of the men became demoralized. Despite these problems, St. Clair continued to advance against the Miami (in what is present-day Indiana). By November 3, his men had arrived on the banks of the Wabash River, near some of the Miami villages. Little Turtle, Blue Jacket, and Tecumseh, aided by British collaborators Alexander McKee and Simon Girty, surprised the poorly-prepared

Americans at Fort Recovery, Ohio, near the headwaters of the Wabash River, with 2000 warriors on November 4, 1791.

Many of the poorly-trained American militiamen immediately fled. St. Clair led the regular soldiers in a bayonet charge and had two horses shot out from under him. Several bullets passed through his clothing, and one took off a lock of his hair.

The natives surrounded the American camp. After three hours of fighting—the remaining Americans fought through the natives as they began a long retreat. The survivors reached Fort Jefferson late that afternoon and evening but with limited quantities of food and supplies there, St. Clair ordered his forces to Fort Washington.

More than half of the Americans were killed or wounded, and the survivors haphazardly fled back to Fort Washington. The battle has since been known as St. Clair's Defeat, the Battle of the Wabash, the Columbia Massacre, or the Battle of a Thousand Slain. It was the most significant defeat of the U.S. Army by natives in American history. Only about fifty natives were killed. St. Clair was among the wounded. One of the survivors stated, "The ground was literally covered with the dead."

A subsequent investigation exonerated St. Clair, but he resigned his army commission in March 1792 at the request of President Washington. However, he continued to serve as the Governor of the Northwest Territory. Eventually, American forces led by General Anthony Wayne won the campaign, overwhelming the natives and resulting in the Treaty of Greenville in 1795.

St. Clair was a Federalist. He hoped to see two states created from the Ohio Territory to increase Federalist power. However, the Democratic-Republicans led by Thomas Jefferson continued to gain influence in the capital and the territory. Despite St. Clair's resistance, the U.S. Congress sanctioned the Enabling Act of 1802 which gave Ohioans the right to form a constitutional convention on the path to statehood. St. Clair remarked the U.S. Congress had no power to interfere in the affairs of those in the Ohio Territory. He also stated the people of the territory "are no more bound by an act of Congress than we would be bound by an edict of the first consul of France." This led to Jefferson removing St. Clair as territorial governor and prevented him from playing a role in organizing the state of Ohio in 1803.

Before George

The grave of Arthur St. Clair

Following his resignation as governor, St. Clair returned to Pennsylvania where he invested in iron mines in the Pittsburgh area and established a foundry to make stoves and castings. He was very liberal with his money, loaning it to friends and family.

Though Congress did pay him a pension of two thousand dollars on May 1, 1810, it was not enough to save St. Clair from financial trouble. He lost his vast landholdings and eventually moved into a small log cabin on the property of his daughter, Louisa St. Clair Robb, on a ridge between Ligonier and Greensburg. He died there on August 31, 1818.

St. Clair was buried in the Old Greensburg Cemetery which later became St. Clair Park in Greensburg, Pennsylvania. His wife Phoebe died shortly after and was buried next to him. A Masonic monument was later placed over their graves. Said the *National Intelligencer* newspaper at the time, "On the summit of the Chestnut Ridge which overlooks the valley of Ligonier, in which the commencement of the revolution found him in prosper; on this lonesome spot, exposed to winter winds, as cold and desolating as the tardy gratitude of his country, died Major General Arthur St. Clair. The traveler as he passed the place, was reminded of the celebrated Roman exile's reply, 'tell the citizens of Rome that you saw Caius Marius sitting amongst the ruins of Carthage.'"

St. Clair remained a controversial figure for years to come, his reputation attached to the defeat on the Wabash. This historian wonders if his reputation would have been different had George Washington lived longer and been able to remind everyone of St. Clair's contributions at Trenton and Princeton.

Arthur St. Clair has been honored in many ways:

- A portion of the Hermitage, St. Clair's home in Oak Grove, Pennsylvania (north of Ligonier), was later moved to Ligonier, Pennsylvania, where it is now preserved, along with St. Clair artifacts and memorabilia at the Fort Ligonier Museum.
- An American Civil War steamer was named USS *St. Clair*.
- The following places were named after him: Upper St. Clair, Pennsylvania; St. Clairsville, Pennsylvania; St. Clair, Schuylkill County, Pennsylvania; St. Clair Township, Westmoreland County, Pennsylvania; East St. Clair Township, Bedford County, Pennsylvania; West St. Clair Township, Bedford County, Pennsylvania; the St. Clair neighborhood in Pittsburgh, Pennsylvania; St. Clair Hospital, Mt. Lebanon, Pennsylvania; St. Clair Township in Butler County, Ohio; St. Clair Township in Columbiana County, Ohio; St. Clairsville, Ohio; St. Clair Avenue in Cleveland, Ohio; Fort St. Clair in Eaton, Ohio; St. Clair County, Illinois; St. Clair County, Missouri; St. Clair County, Alabama; St. Clair Street in Frankfort, Kentucky; and the three-star St. Clair Hotel in Sinclair St., Thurso, Caithness.

Cyrus Griffin
(1748–1810)

"The Last President of Congress"

Buried at Bruton Parish Churchyard,
Williamsburg, Virginia

Cyrus Griffin was an attorney from Farnham, Virginia, who served as a member of the Virginia House of Delegates, the Second Continental Congress, and the Ninth Congress of the Confederation. During the final year of the Continental Congress, Griffin was the last President of Congress, overseeing the transition from the Articles of Confederation to the U.S. Constitution. He was then appointed a federal district judge during the Washington administration and served in that capacity for the rest of his life.

Cyrus Griffin was born on July 16, 1748, in Farnham Parish, along the Rappahannock River, in Virginia, the fourth son of Leroy Griffin, a tobacco farmer, and his wife, Mary Ann (née Bertrand) Griffin, of Huguenot heritage. The Griffin family is believed to be an old Welsh family, possibly descended from the last king of Wales, Llewellyn Griffin, who fell in battle against Edward I of England, in 1282, after a reign of 28 years. The Griffins were early settlers in Virginia, along the tidewater area, in the mid-1600s. Thomas Griffin and his brother Samuel emigrated from Wales and settled along the Rappahannock River. When Samuel returned to Wales to inherit their late brother's estate, Thomas remained.

Cyrus Griffin (1748–1810)

Cyrus Griffin

Leroy Griffin died while Cyrus was a child, leaving a portion of his estate to him. These funds were utilized to educate Cyrus in Great Britain. He studied law in Scotland at the University of Edinburgh and met Lady Christina Stuart, the eldest daughter of Charles Stuart, the Sixth Earl of Traquair, circa 1770. When Charles, the patriarch of one of Scotland's noble families, learned of the relationship, he was furious. Griffin was the son of a "lowly" planter from Virginia and an Episcopalian. The Stuarts were devout Roman Catholics. Consumed by passion, the young couple eloped to London, where Griffin continued his legal studies at the Middle Temple.

John Griffin, their first child, was born in 1771 while the couple was still in England. In 1774, Griffin, who had graduated from law school, returned to Virginia to start his practice. He left Christina and young John behind. He returned the following year as the hostilities of the American Revolution commenced. He sought a dowry from his father-in-law but was unsuccessful. While in England, he worked privately to find a way to reconcile the differences between England and her American colonies. He proposed the following ideas in a letter to his friend Lord Dartmouth in London:

- That the Commissioners be instructed to meet either the whole or any number of those men who compose the Congress at any particular place except Philadelphia.

- That when so met and Ceremonies adjusted, they shall begin from the year 1763 and discuss each separate grievance complained of by America.

- That when any point is fully debated the Meeting shall adjourn to the next day; in the meantime, the Commissioners are to determine with themselves how far or whether they shall totally admit the hardship under consideration; such determination to be sent in writing upon the next morning, and by a special Officer, to the aforesaid delegates sitting to receive the same; the delegates to vote by a majority whether the determination of the Commissioners will be satisfactory.

- That if there should be any points upon which The Commissioners and Delegates cannot perfectly agree those points may be referred to the wisdom of the next parliament, and the Colonies to be heard by Counsel in the said parliament.

- That when all matters are finished at this united convention, the Members of the Congress shall return to Philadelphia, and the said Congress shall instantly dissolve themselves.

Frustrated on both fronts, Griffin took his wife and son with him and returned to Virginia in 1775. The Griffins would later have five additional children, totaling four sons and two daughters.

The young attorney soon became involved in state politics. In 1777, he was elected to the Virginia House of Delegates. Then, on May 29,

1778, he was elected to the Continental Congress. He attended sessions from August 19 to October 21 and about December 23 to December 31, 1778. During this time, he observed the machinations and posturing of members of Congress, writing to Thomas Jefferson about his worries and the perceived lack of honor and patriotism.

Griffin was re-elected to the Continental Congress on June 18, 1779, and served through the year's end. He was corresponding with Benjamin Franklin, who was in France, regarding his dowry's settlement. Franklin had taken up representing Griffin to Charles Stuart. Franklin and Stuart were likely acquainted when Franklin visited Scotland in 1771 with Henry Marchant. Thanks to Franklin, Charles Stuart and his daughter reconciled before his death in 1779. In letters to Franklin, Griffin thanked him for his assistance and worried about the Continental Congress's precarious financial position. He also complained that he is often Virginia's lone representative. Griffin held on, serving through June 1780, when he finally resigned. One of his final letters was to Thomas Jefferson regarding the need to increase the military presence in Virginia as it was invaded by the British.

During his final days in Congress, Griffin was appointed a judge of the Court of Appeals in Cases of Capture, which handled cases involving ships and cargo seized during the war. Griffin served on this court longer than anyone else in its short history, remaining until the Continental Congress ended its jurisdiction in 1787. In 1782, he was one of the committee members appointed by Congress to oversee a settlement of the boundary dispute between Pennsylvania and Connecticut regarding the Wyoming Valley.

Griffin's attempts to return to Congress failed in 1783, 1784, and 1786, when he lost elections. He also failed to gain a seat on the Virginia Executive Council in 1786. However, he did win a seat in the Virginia House of Delegates, which he held until January 1787. Then, on October 23, 1787, Griffin was elected to Congress after the U.S. Constitution had been signed while the state ratification process was underway. Sadly, during this time, his son Cyrus Jr. died.

On January 22, 1788, Griffin was elected the fifteenth and final President of Congress, succeeding Arthur St. Clair. He then presided

Before George

The decrepit stone marking Cyrus Griffin in Williamsburg.

over the Continental Congress's final year as it transitioned to the new constitutional government. His term ended on November 16, 1788.

Griffin lost the election to be a member of the First Congress in the House of Representatives. However, he was elected to the Virginia Executive Council. Before he could take his seat in August 1789, President Washington appointed Griffin to a three-man commission established to negotiate with the Creek Indians. He served on this commission with David Humphreys and Benjamin Lincoln.

Next, Griffin expressed his desire to Washington to become the next U.S. Ambassador to France, succeeding Thomas Jefferson. However, Washington had other ideas. During a Senate recess, he appointed Griffin to be a judge on the newly created United States District Court for the District of Virginia. Washington nominated him again on February 8, 1790, and Griffin was approved by the Senate two days later. He served in this capacity for the remainder of his life. In 1807, Griffin may have attended or presided over the treason trial of Vice President Aaron Burr. He also officiated the libel trial of newspaper editor James T. Callendar, embroiled in controversies against Thomas Jefferson.

Cyrus Griffin died at Yorktown, Virginia, on December 14, 1810, at 62. An article in the Baltimore newspaper *The Federal Republican* stated, "He was a gentleman highly respected for his eminent virtues, his integrity, and independence. He has filled many public appointments, and always with honor to himself, and with advantage to the country."

Griffin was laid to rest next to his wife, who had predeceased him in 1807, in the Bruton Churchyard in Williamsburg, Virginia. Both lie in a nondescript, unmarked tomb.

Charles Thomson
(1729–1824)

"The Secretary of Congress"

Buried at Laurel Hill Cemetery,
Philadelphia, Pennsylvania

Secretary, Continental Congress

Although few people have heard of Charles Thomson, he was one of America's most significant and influential Founding Fathers. He served as the only Secretary of the Continental Congress for its entire fifteen years. He was a tremendous unifying factor. He kept the minutes of all sessions of Congress, including special minutes of all the secret meetings and deals. His journals and files became the archives of our nation. In all the factional disputes of the Revolutionary period, his judgment was respected. During the rumors and uncertainties of the Revolutionary War, Thomson helped the Continental Congress retain the faith and support of the people by insisting that full and honest reports be issued, under his signature, concerning all battles and engagements whether won or lost. His reputation was such that his reports were in high demand. When a congressional paper appeared containing his signature, the expression was frequently heard, "here comes the truth." Thomson's name was regarded as an emblem of truth.

Charles Thomson was born in 1729 in County Derry, Ireland to Scots-Irish parents. He was one of six children, and his mother died in 1739 during or shortly after the birth of his youngest sibling. Within a

Charles Thomson (1729–1824)

Charles Thomson

few months, his father John set out for Philadelphia with Charles and three of his older brothers. John became violently ill and died within sight of the shore. The ship was just off the capes of Delaware. The children were now left to the mercy of the sea captain, who embezzled the money which the father had brought with him and landed the boys ashore at New Castle, Delaware.

There Charles was separated from his brothers. He was placed in the care of a blacksmith who intended to make him an indentured servant. Through good fortune, he was admitted to the New London Academy in Chester County, Pennsylvania. While a student there, Thomson made the acquaintance of Benjamin Franklin and frequently sought his advice regarding the prospects of working in Philadelphia. Franklin, being President of the Board of Trustees of the new Academy of Philadelphia (the forerunner of the University of Pennsylvania), secured a position for Thomson at the school. He started as a tutor there on January 7, 1751.

Before George

He served as a tutor until 1755 and left to become head of the Latin department at Philadelphia's Friends Public School. In 1758 he married Ruth Mather, a member of a well-to-do Chester family. In 1760 he left teaching to enter into business. He and Ruth separated in 1769. In 1770 tragedy struck when their infant twins and Ruth died.

While at the Friends School, Thomson joined the Quakers in their opposition to the Penn family's Indian policy. He became the secretary for the Delaware Indians in 1756 at a great council held in Easton, Pennsylvania to resolve their differences with the settlers. The tribe adopted him as a son according to an ancient Indian custom. All during this time, he was allied with Ben Franklin, but they parted politically during the Stamp Act crisis in 1765. He then allied himself with John Dickinson. He worked diligently throughout the Revolutionary period to keep English goods out of Philadelphia. By 1773 he was writing fiery handbills against the importation of tea from the East India Company. During this decade Thomson was the colony's most powerful protest organizer. He became known as "the Sam Adams of Philadelphia." He also became a leader in Philadelphia's Sons of Liberty, a secret organization of landowners throughout the colonies formed to protect the rights of colonists and to fight taxation by the British government.

On September 1, 1774, Thomson married Hannah Harrison, the sister of Benjamin Harrison, who would become a signer of the Declaration of Independence. The following Monday, September 5, the First Continental Congress convened in Philadelphia and unanimously selected Thomson as Secretary.

He served over the next fifteen years as secretary to the first and second Continental Congresses and then to the Confederation Congress. Through those fifteen years, Congress saw many delegates come and go, but Thomson's dedication to recording the debates and decisions provided continuity. The Continental Congress was in some respects one of the most remarkable legislative bodies the world has ever seen. Thomson knew better than any other man the secret history of Congress and the motives which influenced its members. He beheld the development of national consciousness, and he was present at the dawn of independence. Thomson's name appeared on the first published version

Charles Thomson (1729–1824)

Obelisk honoring Charles Thomson.

of the Declaration of Independence as the only non-delegate signature. He signed in his capacity as Congressional Secretary.

Among his many accomplishments as Secretary, Thomson designed the Great Seal of the United States. The United States of America continues to use the Great Seal on all of its official documents. It can be easily found on the reverse side of the one-dollar bill.

Thomson's service was not without its critics, however. In 1780 delegate James Searle, a close friend of John Adams, began a cane fight on the floor of Congress, claiming that Thomson misquoted him in the minutes. Both men were slashed in the face. Thomson's recordings of events frequently led to arguments and fights on the floor of Congress.

Thomson was keenly aware of the slavery problem. He wrote to Jefferson in 1785: "It grieves me to the soul that there should be such grounds for your apprehensions respecting the irritation that will be produced in the southern states by what you have said of slavery. However, I would not have you discouraged. This is a cancer we must get rid of. It is a blot on our character that must be wiped out. If it cannot be done by religion, reason, and philosophy, confident I am that it will be done one day by blood."

Thomson's last official act as Secretary was to inform George Washington of his election. He traveled to Mt. Vernon on April 1789 to tell him officially that under the new constitution he had been elected the first President. By July, Thomson was retired, having turned over the Great Seal of the United States to Washington.

As Secretary of Congress, Thomson chose what to include in the official journals of the Continental Congress. He also prepared a work of over 1000 pages that covered the political history of the American Revolution. After leaving office, he chose to destroy this work, stating his desire to avoid "contradicting all the histories of the great events of the Revolution. Let the world admire the supposed wisdom and valor of our great men. Perhaps they may adopt the qualities that have been ascribed to them, and thus good may be done. I shall not undeceive future generations."

Charles Thomson died on August 16, 1824, at the age of 95. He had been residing in Bryn Mawr, Pennsylvania at Harriton House which still stands today and operates as a museum. He was initially buried there, but in 1838 his nephew moved his remains to Laurel Hill Cemetery in Philadelphia. A large handsome monument marks his grave.

Appendix A
Terms of the Presidents of Congress

President of Congress	Colony/State	Term Start	Term End	Length
Peyton Randolph	Virginia	September 5, 1774	October 22, 1774	47 days
Henry Middleton	South Carolina	October 22, 1774	October 26, 1774	4 days
(Congress Not In Session)		October 27, 1774	May 9, 1775	195 days
Peyton Randolph	Virginia	May 10, 1775	May 24, 1775	14 days
John Hancock	Massachusetts	May 24, 1775	October 29, 1777	2 years, 158 days
(Vacant)		October 30, 1777	October 31, 1777	2 days
Henry Laurens	South Carolina	November 1, 1777	December 9, 1778	1 year, 38 days
John Jay	New York	December 10, 1778	September 28, 1779	292 days
Samuel Huntington	Connecticut	September 28, 1779	July 10, 1781	1 year, 285 days
Thomas McKean	Delaware	July 10, 1781	November 5, 1781	118 days
John Hanson	Maryland	November 5, 1781	November 4, 1782	364 days
Elias Boudinot	New Jersey	November 4, 1782	November 3, 1783	364 days
Thomas Mifflin	Pennsylvania	November 3, 1783	June 3, 1784	213 days
(Vacant)		June 4, 1784	November 29, 1784	179 days
Richard Henry Lee	Virginia	November 30, 1784	November 4, 1785	339 days
(Vacant)		November 5, 1785	November 22, 1785	18 days
John Hancock	Massachusetts	November 23, 1785	June 5, 1786	194 days
Nathaniel Gorham	Massachusetts	June 6, 1786	February 2, 1787	241 days
Arthur St. Clair	Pennsylvania	February 2, 1787	November 4, 1787	275 days
(Vacant)		November 5, 1787	January 21, 1788	78 days
Cyrus Griffin	Virginia	January 22, 1788	November 2, 1788	298 days
(Vacant)		November 3, 1788	April 30, 1789	179 days

Secretary of Congress	Colony/State	Term Start	Term End	Length
Charles Thomson	Pennsylvania	September 5, 1774	July 23, 1789	14 years 322 days

* During the times when there was a vacancy for the President of Congress, the Secretary of Congress was the senior officer, continuing to manage the paperwork and records of the country. This means that Charles Thomson fulfilled this role, unofficially, for a period of 1 yr., 91 days. Following Washington's inauguration, Thomson spent the next three months transitioning his role until The Great Seal was transferred.

Appendix B
The Articles of Confederation Regarding the Role of President

The United States, in congress assembled, shall have authority to appoint a committee, to sit in the recess of congress, to be denominated, "A Committee of the States," and to consist of one delegate from each State; and to appoint such other committees and civil officers as may be necessary for managing the general affairs of the united states under their direction – to appoint one of their number to preside; provided that no person be allowed to serve in **the office of president** more than one year in any term of three years; to ascertain the necessary sums of money to be raised for the service of the united states, and to appropriate and apply the same for defraying the public expenses; to borrow money or emit bills on the credit of the united states, transmitting every half year to the respective states an account of the sums of money so borrowed or emitted, – to build and equip a navy – to agree upon the number of land forces, and to make requisitions from each state for its quota, in proportion to the number of white inhabitants in such state, which requisition shall be binding; and thereupon the legislature of each state shall appoint the regimental officers, raise the men, and clothe, arm, and equip them, in a soldier-like manner, at the expense of the united states; and the officers and men so clothed, armed, and equipped, shall march to the place appointed, and within the time agreed on by the united states, in congress assembled; but if the united states, in congress assembled, shall, on consideration of circumstances, judge proper that any state should not raise men, or should raise a smaller number than its quota, and that any other state should raise a greater number of men than the quota thereof, such extra number shall be raised, officered, clothed, armed, and equipped in the same manner as the quota of such state, unless the legislature of such state shall judge that such extra number cannot be safely spared out of the same, in which case they shall raise, officer, clothe, arm, and equip, as many of such extra number as they judge can be safely spared. And the officers and men so clothed, armed, and equipped, shall march to the place appointed, and within the time agreed on by the united states in congress assembled.

Sources

Books, Magazines, Journals, Files:

Alexander, Edward P. *Revolutionary Conservative: James Duane of New York*. New York: Ams Press, 1978.

Anthony, Katharine Susan. *First Lady of the Revolution; The Life of Mercy Otis Warren*. Port Washington, N.Y.: Kennikat Press, 1972.

Appleby, Joyce. *Inheriting the Revolution: The First Generation of Americans*. Cambridge, Massachusetts: Harvard University Press, 2000.

Atkinson, Rick. *The British Are Coming: The War for America, Lexington to Princeton, 1775-1777*. New York: Henry Holt & Co. 2019.

Bordewich, Fergus M. *The First Congress: How James Madison, George Washington, and a Group of Extraordinary Men Invented the Government*. New York: Simon and Schuster Paperbacks, 2016.

Boudreau, George W. *Independence: A Guide to Historic Philadelphia*. Yardley, Pennsylvania: Westholme Publishing, LLC. 2012.

Bowen, Catherine Drinker. *Miracle at Philadelphia: The Story of the Constitutional Convention May to September 1787*. Boston, Massachusetts: Little, Brown & Company, 1966.

Breen, T.H, *George Washington's Journey: The President Forges a New Nation*. New York: Simon & Schuster. 2016.

Brookhiser, Richard. *Gentleman Revolutionary: Gouverneur Morris The Rake Who Wrote the Constitution*. New York: Free Press, 2003.

———. *John Marshall: The Man Who Made the Supreme Court*. New York: Basic Books. 2018.

Brush, Edward Hale. *Rufus King and His Times*. New York: N.L. Brown, 1926.

Chadwick, Bruce. I Am Murdered: *George Wythe, Thomas Jefferson, and the Killing That Shocked a New Nation*. Hoboken, New Jersey: John Wiley & Sons, 2009.

Chambers, II, John Whiteclay. *The Oxford Companion to American Military History*. Oxford: Oxford University Press, 1999.

Commager, Henry Steele & Richard B. Morris. *The Spirit of 'Seventy-Six: The Story of the American Revolution as Told by Participants*. New York: Harper & Rowe, 1967.

Cole, Ryan. *Light-Horse Harry Lee: The Rise and Fall of a Revolutionary Hero*. Washington, D.C.: Regnery History. 2019.

Conlin, Joseph R. *The Morrow Book of Quotations in American History*. New York: William Morrow and Company, Inc., 1984.

Daniels, Jonathan. *Ordeal of Ambition*. Garden City, New York: Doubleday & Company, Inc., 1970.

Dann, John C. *The Revolution Remembered: Eyewitness Accounts of the War for Independence*. Chicago: University of Chicago Press, 1980.

DeRose, Chris. *Founding Rivals: Madison vs. Monroe: The Bill of Rights and the Election that Saved a Nation*. New York: MJF Books, 2011.

Drury, Bob & Tom Clavin. *Valley Forge*. New York: Simon & Schuster. 2018.

Ellis, Joseph J. *Revolutionary Summer: The Birth of American Independence*. New York: Alfred A. Knopf, 2013.

———. *The Quartet: Orchestrating the Second American Revolution, 1783-1789*. New York: Alfred A. Knopf, 2015.

———. *His Excellency: George Washington*. New York: Alfred A. Knopf, 2004.

Flexner, James Thomas. *George Washington in the American Revolution, 1775-1783*. Boston: Little, Brown & Company, 1967.

Flower, Lenore Embick. "Visit of President George Washington to Carlisle, 1794." Carlisle, Pennsylvania: The Hamilton Library and Cumberland County Historical Society, 1932.

Gerlach, Don R. *Proud Patriot: Philip Schuyler and the War of Independence, 1775-1783*. Syracuse, N.Y.: Syracuse University Press, 1987.

Goodrich, Charles A. *Lives of the Signers of the Declaration of Independence*. Charlotteville, N.Y.: SamHar Press, 1976.

Griffith, IV, William R. *The Battle of Lake George: England's First Triumph in the French and Indian War*. Charleston, South Carolina: The History Press, 2016.

Grossman, Mark. *Encyclopedia of the Continental Congress*. Armenia, New York: Grey House Publishing, 2015.

Hamilton, Edward P. *Fort Ticonderoga: Key to a Continent*. Boston: Little, Brown & Company, 1964.

Isenberg, Nancy. *Fallen Founder: The Life of Aaron Burr*. New York: Penguin Group, 2007.

Kennedy, Roger G. *Burr, Hamilton, and Jefferson: A Study in Character*. New York: Oxford University Press, 1999.

Kiernan, Denise & Joseph D'Agnese. *Signing Their Lives Away: The Fame and Misfortune of the Men Who Signed the Declaration of Independence*. Philadelphia: Quirk Books, 2008.

———. *Signing Their Rights Away: The Fame and Misfortune of the Men Who Signed the United States Constitution*. Philadelphia: Quirk Books, 2011.

Klarman, Michael J. *The Framers' Coup: The Making of the United States Constitution*. New York: Oxford University Press, 2016.

Langguth, A. J. *Patriots*. New York: Simon and Schuster, 1988.

Larson, Edward J. *A Magnificent Catastrophe*. New York: Free Press, 2007.

Lee, Mike. Written *Out of History: The Forgotten Founders Who Fought Big Government*. New York: Penguin Books, 2017.

Lewis, James E., Jr., *The Burr Conspiracy: Uncovering the Story of an Early American Crisis*, Princeton: Princeton University Press, 2017.

Lockridge, Ross Franklin. *The Harrisons*. 1941.

Lomask, Milton. *Aaron Burr: The Years from Princeton to Vice President, 1756-1805*. New York: Farrar Straus Giroux, 1979.

Lossing, Benson J. *Pictorial Field Book of the Revolution*. New York: Harper Brothers. 1851.

Sources

Maier, Pauline. *American Scripture: Making the Declaration of Independence.* New York: Alfred A. Knopf, Inc., 1997.

McCullough, David. *John Adams.* New York: Simon & Schuster, 2002.

Meltzer, Brad & Josh Mensch. *The First Conspiracy: The Secret Plot to Kill George Washington.* New York: Flat Iron Books. 2018.

Middlekauff, Robert. *The Glorious Cause: The American Revolution, 1763-1789.* Oxford: Oxford University Press, 2005.

Miller, Jr., Arthur P. & Marjorie L. Miller. *Pennsylvania Battlefields and Military Landmarks.* Mechanicsburg, Pennsylvania: Stackpole Books, 2000.

Millett, Allan R. & Peter Maslowski. *For the Common Defense: A Military History of the United States of America.* New York: The Free Press, 1984.

Moore, Charles. *The Family Life of George Washington.* New York: Houghton Mifflin, 1926.

Nagel, Paul C. *The Lees of Virginia: Seven Generations of an American Family.* Oxford: Oxford University Press, 1990.

O'Connell, Robert L. *Revolutionary: George Washington at War.* New York: Random House. 2019.

Racove, Jack N. *Revolutionaries: A New History of the Invention of America.* New York: Houghton Mifflin Harcourt, 2011.

Raphael, Ray. *Founding Myths: Stories That Hide Our Patriotic Past.* New York: MJF Books, 2004.

Rossiter, Clinton. *1787 The Grand Convention.* New York: The Macmillan Company, 1966.

Seymour, Joseph. *The Pennsylvania Associators, 1747-1777.* Yardley, Pennsylvania: Westholme Publishing, LLC. 2012.

Schweikart, Larry & Michael Allen. *A Patriot's History of the United States from Columbus's Great Discovery to the War on Terror.* New York: Penguin, 2004.

Sharp, Arthur G. *Not Your Father's Founders.* Avon, Massachusetts: Adams Media, 2012.

Stahr, Walter. *John Jay: Founding Father.* New York: Diversion Books, 2017.

Taafee, Stephen R. *The Philadelphia Campaign, 1777-1778.* Lawrence, Kansas: University of Kansas Press, 2003.

Tinkcom, Harry Marlin, *The Republicans and the Federalists in Pennsylvania, 1790-1801.* Harrisburg, Pennsylvania: Pennsylvania Historical and Museum Commission. 1950.

Ward, Matthew C. *Breaking the Backcountry: The Seven Years' War in Virginia and Pennsylvania, 1754-1765.* Pittsburgh, Pennsylvania: University of Pittsburgh Press, 2003.

Weisberger, Bernard A. *America Afire: Jefferson, Adams, and the Revolutionary Election of 1800.* New York: HarperCollins, 2000.

Wood, Gordon S. *The Radicalism of the American Revolution.* New York: Vintage Books, 1993.

———. *Empire of Liberty: A History of the Early Republic, 1789-1815.* New York: Penguin Books, 2004.

———. *Revolutionary Characters: What Made the Founders Different.* New York: Penguin Books, 2006.

———. *The Americanization of Benjamin Franklin*. Oxford: Oxford University Press, 2009.

Wright, Benjamin F. *The Federalist: The Famous Papers on the Principles of American Government: Alexander Hamilton, James Madison, John Jay*. New York: Metro Books, 2002.

Zobel, Hiller B. *The Boston Massacre*. New York: W. W. Norton & Company, 1970.

Video Resources:

Guelzo, Allen C. The Great Courses: *America's Founding Fathers* (Course N. 8525). Chantilly, Virginia: The Teaching Company, 2017.

Online Resources:

Archives.gov – for information on the Constitutional Convention.
CauseofLiberty.blogspot.com – for information on Daniel Carroll.
ColonialHall.com – for information about the signers of the Declaration of Independence.
DSDI1776.com – for information on many Founders.
FamousAmericans.net – for information on many Founders.
FindaGrave.com – for burial information, vital statistics and obituaries.
FirstLadies.org – for information on Abigail Adams.
Newspapers.com – Hundreds of newspaper articles were accessed—too numerous to mention here.
NPS.gov – for information on various park sites.
TeachingAmericanHistory.com – for information on Charles Pinckney and George Wythe.
TheHistoryJunkie.com – for information on multiple Founders.
USHistory.org – for information on multiple Founders.
Wikipedia.com – for general historical information.

Index

Academy of Philadelphia, 95
Adams, John, 11, 16, 21, 35-37, 41, 51, 53, 74-75, 97
Adams, Samuel, 16, 20-23, 74, 96
Addison Burial Ground, 54, 57
American Antiquarian Society, 64
American Bible Society, 64
American Board of Commissioners for Foreign Missions, 65
American Philosophical Society, 27
Amherst, Jeffrey, 82
Armitage, Sarah, 50
Arnold, Benedict, 69
Articles of Confederation, 3, 5-6, 19, 22, 25, 27, 32, 38, 43, 45, 48, 51, 54, 56, 63, 71, 74, 78, 88
Aylett, Anne, 72

Ball, Eleanor, 26
Baltimore, Maryland, 68
Bayard, Phoebe, 82
Berkeley Plantation, 8
Bland, Richard, 10, 74
Blue Jacket, 84
Borden, Mary, 50
Boston Latin School, 19
Boston, Massachusetts, 19, 21, 23, 34-35, 56, 77, 82
Boston Massacre, 21, 23
Boston Tea Party, 21, 34
Botetourt, Lord, 10
Boudinot, Annis, 59
Boudinot, Elias (father), 59
Boudinot, Elias, 5, 57, 59-65
Boudinot, Elias (Cherokee), 65
Boudinot, Elisha, 59
Boudinot, Mary Catherine, 59
Boudinot, Susan, 60, 64
Bowdoin, James, 23, 82
Braddock's Defeat, 9, 72
Bradford, William, 63
Braintree, Massachusetts, 19
Braxton, Carter, 10, 12
Briscoe, John Hanson, 58
Bruton Parish Churchyard, 88, 93
Bryn Mawr, Pennsylvania, 98
Bull, Mary Henrietta, 15
Bull, William, 15
Bunce Island, 26

Burgoyne, General, 62
Burlington, New Jersey, 59, 65
Burnt House Field Plantation, 71, 73, 76
Burr, Aaron, 40, 93

Call, Rebecca, 77
Callendar, James T., 93
Campbell, Arthur, 76
Carr, Dabney, 74
Carroll, Daniel, 56
Cary, Archibald, 74
Castle William, 21
Chantilly-on-the-Potomac, 72
Charleston, South Carolina, 14, 17, 25-26
Charlestown, Massachusetts, 77, 80
Cherokee, 27, 65
Cincinnati, Ohio, 64-65, 84
Clinton, George, 38-40
Coffin, Nathaniel, 77
Coles Point, Virginia, 71, 73, 76
College of William and Mary, 7-8, 11-12
College of Philadelphia, 67
Colonial Cemetery, 43, 47
Columbia University, 33
Concord, Massachusetts, 1, 10, 60, 67, 74
Constitution, 4, 6, 23, 29, 32, 38-39, 45, 51, 63, 66, 70, 77, 79, 88, 90
Contee, Jane, 54
Continental Association, 2, 7, 14, 32, 35, 66, 71, 74
Conway, Thomas, 69
Cooper River, 26, 29
Cooper, Samuel, 75
Cornwallis, Lord, 28
County Derry, Ireland, 94
Cresap, Michael, 56

Dartmouth, Lord, 90
Deane, Silas, 74-75
Declaration of Independence, 2, 5, 8, 14, 16, 19, 22, 36, 43, 47-48, 51, 71, 74, 96-97
Devotion, Ebenezer, 44
Devotion, Martha, 44
Dickinson, John, 16, 96
Digges, Dudley, 74
Dinwiddie, Robert, 9
Dover, Delaware, 50
Dunmore, Lord, 10-11, 16

Easton, Pennsylvania, 96
Elizabeth, New Jersey, 60

Fairfield, Connecticut, 22
Farnham, Virginia, 88
Federalist Papers, 32, 38
First Presbyterian Church Cemetery, 53
Fort Hamilton, 84
Fort Jefferson, 84-85
Fort Pitt, 83
Fort Recovery, Ohio, 85
Fort Ticonderoga, 83
Fort Washington, 56, 85
Fort Wayne, Indiana, 84
Franklin, Benjamin, 11, 16, 37, 59, 74, 91, 95-96
Frederick, Maryland, 58
French and Indian War, 9, 72

Gadsden, Christopher, 15
Gage, Thomas, 16, 22
Gates, Horatio, 69
Girty, Simon, 84
Gooch, William, 9
Goose Creek, South Carolina, 14, 17-18
Gorham, Mary, 77
Gorham, Nathaniel (father), 77
Gorham, Nathaniel, 77-80, 84
Granary Burial Ground, 19, 23-24
Greensburg, Pennsylvania, 81, 86
Griffin, Cyrus, 5, 88-93
Griffin, Cyrus (son), 91
Griffin, John, 89-90
Griffin, Leroy, 88
Griffin, Mary Ann, 88
Griffin, Samuel, 88
Griffin, Thomas, 88

Hague, Westmoreland County, Virginia, 71
Hamilton, Alexander, 38
Hanbury, John, 8
Hancock, John (father), 19
Hancock, John, 3, 5, 10, 16, 19-24, 74, 76, 78
Hancock, John George Washington, 22
Hancock, Lydia, 19, 22
Hancock Manor, 19-20
Hancock, Thomas, 19-20
Hanson, Alexander Contee, 58
Hanson, Elizabeth, 54
Hanson, Jane Contee, 58
Hanson, John, 5, 54-58, 63
Hanson, Peter Contee, 56, 58
Hanson, Samuel, 54
Harmar, Josiah, 84
Harrison, Benjamin, 8, 10, 74, 96
Harrison, Elizabeth, 8
Harrison, Sarah, 96

Harriton House, 98
Hartley, David, 37
Harvard University, 19
Henry, Patrick, 9-10, 74
Hillsborough, Lord, 28
House of Hancock, 20
Howe, General, 61
Howland, John, 77
Humphreys, David, 92
Hunter, William, 82
Huntington, Mehetabel, 43
Huntington, Nathaniel, 43
Huntington, Samuel, 43-47, 56
Huntington, Samuel (son), 44
Huntington, Susan, 46
Hutchinson, Thomas, 21-22

Jay, John, 32-42, 45
Jay, Mary, 33
Jay, Peter, 32
Jay Treaty, 40
Jefferson, Thomas, 9-11, 40, 74, 85, 91-93, 98
John Jay Cemetery, 32, 42
Johnston, Samuel, 56

Knox, Henry, 84

Lancaster, Pennsylvania, 66, 69-70
Laurel Hill Cemetery, 48, 53, 94, 98
Laurens Family Cemetery, 25
   Laurens, Henry, 5, 25-31, 37, 75
Laurens, Henry (son), 29
Laurens, Hester, 25
Laurens, Jean Samuel, 25
Laurens, John, 27-30
Laurens, Martha, 27
Lee, Arthur, 74
Lee Family Plot, 71, 75-76
Lee, Francis Lightfoot, 71, 73-74
Lee, Hannah Harrison, 71
Lee, "Light Horse Harry," 71
Lee, Phillip, 72-73
Lee Resolution, 71, 74
Lee, Richard Henry, 10, 71-76
Lee, Thomas, 71
Lee, Thomas Ludwell, 73
Lexington, Massachusetts, 1, 10, 22, 60, 67, 74
Liberty, 21
Ligonier, Pennsylvania, 86-87
Lincoln, Benjamin, 83, 92
Little Turtle, 84
Livingston, Philip, 49
Livingston, Robert, 33, 74
Livingston, Sarah, 34, 36, 42
Livingston, William, 34, 61
Long Island, 61, 68

Index

Louisburg, Nova Scotia, 82
Lynch, Thomas, 15

Machadoc Plantation, 71
Madison, James, 38, 40
Marbury v. Madison, 39
Marchant, Henry, 91
Marshall, John, 39, 41
Mather, Ruth, 96
Mayflower, 77
Mayflower Compact, 77
McKean, Thomas, 5, 48-53, 56-57
McKee, Alexander, 84
McKenzie, Mary, 15
Mepkin, 28-29
Middle Temple of Gray's Inn, 8, 89
Middleton, Arthur (father), 14
Middleton, Arthur (son), 14, 16
Middleton, Henry, 10, 14-18
Middleton Place, 15
Middleton, Sarah, 14
Middleton, Susannah, 17
Mifflin, Thomas, 6, 66-70, 76
Moncks Corner, South Carolina, 25, 29
Morris, Gouverneur, 34
Morris, Robert, 74
Morris, Sarah, 67
Mount Vernon, 98
Mulberry Grove Plantation, 54

Nassau Hall, 63
New Castle, Delaware, 49, 95
New London, Connecticut, 77
New London Academy, 95
New London Township, Chester County, Pennsylvania, 48
New York Manumission Society, 40
New York, New York, 25, 32-34, 37, 39, 51, 61, 68
Newport, Rhode Island, 22
Nicholas, Robert Carter, 74
North, Lord, 10
Northwest Territory, 5, 57, 81, 84-85
Norwich, Connecticut, 43, 47

Ogden, Robert, 50
Old Greensburg Cemetery, 86
Old Norwichtown Cemetery, 43, 47
Olive Branch Petition, 2
Oswald, Richard, 26, 28-29, 37
Otis, James, 21
Oxon Hill, Maryland, 54, 57
Packard, Anne Gaskins, 74
Paine, Robert Treat, 16
Paine, Thomas, 64
Parker, John, 17
Pendleton, Edmund, 10, 74

Phelps, Oliver, 80
Philadelphia, Pennsylvania, 2, 5, 10-12, 22, 27-28, 34-35, 48, 50, 53, 56-57, 59, 61-63, 65, 67, 79, 94-95, 98
Phipps Street Cemetery, 77, 80
Pittsburgh, Pennsylvania, 86
Port Tobacco Parish, Charles County, Maryland, 54
Poughkeepsie, New York, 38
Price, Thomas, 56
Princeton, New Jersey, 59, 63, 65, 68, 83, 87
Princeton University, 64
Prussian Scheme, 78-79

Quincy, Dorothy (Dolly), 22
Quincy, Massachusetts, 19, 36

Raleigh Tavern, 10
Ramsay, David, 27
Randolph, Beverly, 7
Randolph, John (father), 7, 13
Randolph, John (brother), 8-9
Randolph, Mary, 7
Randolph, Peyton, 5, 7-13, 16, 74
Randolph, Susannah, 7, 13
Randolph, Thomas, 7
Read, George, 50-51
Revere, Paul, 21-22, 35
Rittenhouse, David, 63
Robb, Louisa St. Clair, 86
Robinson, John, 9
Rodney, Cesar, 49-50
Ruggles, Timothy, 49-50
Rutledge, Edward, 15
Rutledge, John, 15, 49
Rye, New York, 32-33, 42

St. Clair, Arthur, 5, 81-87, 91
St. Clair Park, 81, 86
St. James Goose Creek Cemetery, 14, 17-18
St. Mary's Episcopal Churchyard, 59, 65
Scotland, Connecticut, 43
Searle, James, 98
Shay's Rebellion, 23, 78-79, 84
Sherman, Roger, 45, 74
Sinclair, Elizabeth, 82
Sinclair, William, 82
Sons of Liberty, 21, 96
Staten Island, 25, 61
Stockton, Hannah, 60, 64
Stockton, Richard, 59, 61
Stratford Hall, 71-72
Stuart, Charles, 89-91
Stuart, Lady Christina, 89-91
Suffolk Resolves, 35

Tazewell Hall, 7

Tecumseh, 84
The Oakes, 14-16
Thomson, Charles, 3, 5, 34, 94-98
Thomas, John, 95
Thurso, Scotland, 81
Tower of London, 25, 28
Treaty of Fort Harmar, 84
Treaty of Greenville, 85
Treaty of Paris, 5, 28-29, 32, 37, 59, 69
Trenton, New Jersey, 68-69, 83, 87
Trinity Lutheran Church, 66, 69-70
Tubman, Harriet, 58

Uwatie, Gallegina, 65

Valley Forge, Pennsylvania, 68
von Steuben, Baron, 79

Wakefield Academy, 71
Walcott, Oliver, 45

Washington, D.C., 58
Washington, George, 1, 4, 6, 9-10, 32, 36, 39-40,
    45, 51, 56-57, 59, 61-63, 66, 69-70, 74, 83,
    85, 87-88, 92, 98
Watie, Buck, 65
Wayne, Anthony, 85
Wharton, Thomas, 70
Wickling, Elizabeth, 25
Williams, John, 15
Williams, Mary Baker, 15
Williamsburg, Virginia, 7-8, 10, 12, 88, 92-93
Witherspoon, John, 60
Wolfe, James, 82
Woodward Hill Cemetery, 70
Wren Chapel, 7, 11-13
Wythe, George, 9

Yale College, 43
York, Pennsylvania, 27, 62
Yorktown, Virginia, 5, 28, 54, 57, 83, 93

WE THE PEOPLE OF THE UNITED STATES, in Order to form a more perfect Union, establish Justice, insure domestic Tranquility, provide for the common defense, promote the general Welfare, and secure the Blessings of Liberty to ourselves and our Posterity, do ordain and establish this Constitution for the United States of America.

www.ingramcontent.com/pod-product-compliance
Lightning Source LLC
Chambersburg PA
CBHW010856090426
42737CB00019B/3386